African Film Studies

African Film Studies is an accessible and engaging introduction to African cinemas, showcasing the diverse cinematic expressions across the continent. Bringing African cinemas out of the margins and into mainstream film studies, the book provides a succinct overview of the history, aesthetics, and theory of sub-Saharan African cinematic productions.

Updated throughout, this new edition includes new chapters on Nollywood, Ethiopian cinema, streaming, and the rise of televisual series, which serve to complement the book's main themes:

- Overview of African cinemas: Questions assumptions and defines the characteristics of African cinemas across linguistic, geographic, and filmic divides.
- History of African cinemas: Spans the history of film in Africa from colonial import and 'appropriation of the gaze,' the rise of Nollywood and local TV series to streaming, as well as building connections with the development of African American cinema.
- Aesthetics: Introduces new research on previously under-explored aesthetic dimensions such as cinematography, animation, and film music.
- Theoretical approaches: Addresses a number of theoretical approaches and critical frameworks developed by scholars in the study of African cinemas.
- Traditions and practices in African screen media: Features Ethiopian cinema, Nollywood, local televisual series in Burkina Faso and South Africa, and the streaming rush for Africa.

All chapters include case studies, suggestions for further reading, and screening lists to deepen the reader's knowledge, with no prior knowledge of African cinemas required. Students, teachers, and general film enthusiasts would all benefit from this accessible and engaging book.

Boukary Sawadogo is an Associate Professor of Cinema Studies at the City University of New York's City College and CUNY Graduate Center. As a specialist in African cinemas, he has published extensively through film reviews, articles, book chapters, and three books. Since 2020, he is the founding director of Harlem African Animation Festival.

African Film Studies

An Introduction

Second Edition

Boukary Sawadogo

Routledge
Taylor & Francis Group

LONDON AND NEW YORK

Designed cover image: Boukary Sawadogo

Second edition published 2023
by Routledge
4 Park Square, Milton Park, Abingdon, Oxon, OX14 4RN

and by Routledge
605 Third Avenue, New York, NY 10158

Routledge is an imprint of the Taylor & Francis Group, an informa business

© 2023 Boukary Sawadogo

First edition published by Routledge 2019

British Library Cataloguing-in-Publication Data
A catalogue record for this book is available from the British Library

Library of Congress Cataloging-in-Publication Data
Names: Sawadogo, Boukary, author. Title: African film studies: an introduction/
Boukary Sawadogo.
Description: 2 Edition. | New York, NY: Routledge, 2023. | Revised edition of the
author's African film studies, 2019. | Includes bibliographical references and index. |
Summary: "African Film Studies is an accessible and engaging introduction to African
cinemas, showcasing the diverse cinematic expressions across the continent. Bringing
African cinemas out of the margins and into mainstream film studies, the book
provides a succinct overview of the history, aesthetics, and theory of sub-Saharan
African cinematic productions. Updated throughout, this new edition includes new
chapters on Nollywood, Ethiopian cinema, Streaming, and the rise of televisual
series, which serve to complement the book's main themes: Overview of African
cinema(s): Questions assumptions and defines the characteristics of African cinemas
across linguistic, geographic, and filmic divides. History of African cinemas: Spans
the history of film in Africa from colonial import and 'appropriation of the gaze', the
rise of Nollywood and local TV series to streaming, as well as building connections
with the development of African American cinema. Aesthetics: Introduces new
research on previously under-explored aesthetic dimensions such as cinematography,
animation, and film music. Theoretical Approaches: Addresses a number of theoretical
approaches and critical frameworks developed by scholars in the study of African
cinemas. Traditions and practices in African screen media: Features Ethiopian
cinema, Nollywood, Local Televisual Series in Burkina Faso and South Africa,
and the Streaming rush for Africa. All chapters include case studies, suggestions
for further reading, and screening lists to deepen the reader's knowledge, with no
prior knowledge of African cinemas required. Students, teachers, and general film
enthusiasts would all benefit from this accessible and engaging book"– Provided by
publisher.
Identifiers: LCCN 2022034020 | ISBN 9781032160252 (hardback) |
ISBN 9781032160238 (paperback) | ISBN 9781003246763 (ebook)
Subjects: LCSH: Motion pictures–Africa, Sub-Saharan. | Motion pictures–Study and
teaching–Africa, Sub-Saharan. Classification: LCC PN1993.5.A357 S29 2023 |
DDC 791.430967–dc23/eng/20220721
LC record available at https://lccn.loc.gov/2022034020

ISBN: 978-1-032-16025-2 (hbk)
ISBN: 978-1-032-16023-8 (pbk)
ISBN: 978-1-003-24676-3 (ebk)

DOI: 10.4324/9781003246763

Typeset in Bembo
by Deanta Global Publishing Services, Chennai, India

Contents

Figures

Introduction

How I Came to African Cinemas

My journey to African cinemas is that of a scholar-practitioner and a festival founding director. I came to African cinemas as someone who grew up watching Burkinabe films on television and movie theaters in the 1990s, a time that is the tail end of what is considered the golden decade of Burkinabe cinema. These films were by cineastes such as Idrissa Ouedraogo, Gaston Kabore, and Dani Kouyate. I grew up attending biannual editions of FESPACO (Festival Panafricain du Cinéma et de la Télévision de Ouagadougou [Panafrican Film and Television Festival of Ouagadougou]), which opened a window for me to cinematic productions from other African countries and the diaspora. Burkinabe and African films on television and in movie theaters were exceptions in the mass of foreign films—Hollywood, Bollywood, Chinese martial arts movies, Hong Kong action films, and European and Latin American TV serials. My initial encounter and engagement with African films were against the backdrop of foreign productions dominating television and movie screens in Burkina Faso. Years later, I, as was the case with many African-born scholars of African cinemas, had to leave the continent to pursue doctoral studies in which to specialize in productions from Africa. My path led me to the United States. There is a dearth of degree-granting graduate programs on African cinema on the continent. So films are produced in Africa or the Global South in general while teaching and the production and dissemination of critical knowledge tend to come from the West. However, there are indications that this structural imbalance has started to reverse. More film schools have been created since the mid-2000s to locally train professionals in filmmaking techniques, but educational and teaching materials on or about African cinemas are still not widely produced and circulated except for scholarly productions that are mostly designed as conversations between scholars. Educational

Figure 0.0 Boukary Sawadogo, editor of the textbook. Courtesy of Boukary Sawadogo.

resources to engage African cinemas from the classroom floor are much needed. The reversal of the structural imbalance is also happening with locally produced content becoming widely available to African audiences, ushering in a new era.

Now, I would like to ask the reader to make an exercise of self-reflection. Please take a moment to reflect on your own journey to/in African cinemas or your first encounter, and how in hindsight this brings into focus larger questions such as accessibility of films, sustainable film industries in Africa, fields of scholarship and study on the margin, creation and dissemination of critical knowledge, decolonization of curricula, and film function in relation to identity and expanding horizons.

African cinemas are growing, expanding, and diversifying in so many interesting and insightful ways that they should be accessibly studied, taught, and talked about in different spaces. African cinemas are the youngest and least known among the different cinematic traditions and practices in the world. And yet, its massive growth potential will make any scholar, practitioner, cinephile pause to think. The film and audio-visual industry has the potential to create 20 million jobs and generate $20 billion in revenues every year, according to the UNESCO report *The African Film Industry: Trends, Challenges and Opportunities for Growth*, launched in October 2021.

Building on the first edition of *African Film Studies: An Introduction*, this new and expanded edition of the textbook is in response to feedback from users of the first edition, requiring updates to case studies and information in the chapters. Also, a new edition is required to cover more areas in the study and teaching of African cinema through the addition of four new chapters. These chapters include "Ethiopian Cinema," "Nollywood: A Popular and Commercial Cinema," "The Rise of Local African TV Serials: The Case of Burkina Faso and South Africa," and "The Streaming Rush for Africa." In addition, the second edition seeks to rebalance and ease the flow of chapters. The first edition chapters are very engaged with film aesthetics. The new chapters are more narrative in focus with less attention to stylistic elements such as framing, sound, editing, lighting, and animation.

The African film studies textbook project initially grew out of my experience teaching undergraduate and graduate courses in film history and theory, African cinema, and African American cinema at the City University of New York's City College and Graduate Center. In my teaching, I always strive to expose students to a wide range of cinematic traditions and practices beyond Hollywood. My efforts are often stymied by the dearth of teaching or learning resources that are accessible to undergraduate students who do not yet have a solid theoretical background or enough contextual information to fully understand the arguments of existing scholarly monographs on African cinema. The high school textbook *Teaching African Cinema: Video and Teachers Book* (1998) by Roy Ashbury, Wendy Helsby, and Maureen O'Brien, and articles such as "African Films in the Classroom" (2010) by Josef Gugler and "Teaching Women in African Cinema" (2016) by Beti Ellerson appear to be among the very few available teaching and learning materials. There is currently no college-level textbook of African cinemas, in contrast to the myriad of textbook titles on film and media studies that offer, at best, limited remarks on African cinemas in the space of a few paragraphs. In this context, I have started developing materials in my course preparations of sections on African cinemas, particularly addressing African film history, aesthetics, and criticism. What textbook to assign to courses on African cinemas or courses that hold some exploratory interest in African cinema? Considering the existing titles on the market, the answer to this interrogation is anything but straightforward. As a result, I sought to create this educational resource as a comprehensive and student-friendly introductory textbook, which, by extension, could also serve as a resource to teachers with no prior encounter with African cinemas. It is not the textbook's aim and scope to engage African cinemas as a discursive object of conversation among scholars, but rather engage it from the classroom floor as a teaching and learning resource for anyone with little or no prior experience with African cinemas. For the reader already knowledgeable in African cinemas, seeking, for instance, to trace the development of a new theory or specialists' debates on African cinemas, this book may not meet his or her expectations because it is conceived and presented as an introductory educational resource for undergraduates and teachers who are relative novices in the field. And maybe beyond the classroom settings, this educational resource will also find its way into the hands of film enthusiasts in the general public. As beginners, we very often need curated information to ease us into a discipline or field that is new to us. As is sometimes experienced in the process of researching on a new subject of interest, we can easily be overwhelmed with the sizable amount of information upon a first attempt. Sifting through the enormous information could be a daunting task, yet not impossible. This could likely dampen the initial enthusiasm or intellectual curiosity that prompted the first contact, which may in turn cause us to cease any further pursuit in the area of interest out of frustration or lack of guidance. In this respect, this textbook is rightly intended to provide the reader with that guidance into African film studies, an introductory step that will enable the reader to get a bird's-eye view of the field or a foundational knowledge to pursue research in areas of interest.

The two overarching goals of the textbook are for undergraduates and instructors of introductory or special topics courses on African cinemas to have an accessible academic resource at their disposal, and also to increase the visibility of African cinemas in the larger field of film and media studies. In this respect, the book offers an approach to the study and teaching of African cinemas that is grounded in the field of film studies instead of textual interpretations from other disciplines such as literature, languages, sociology, or anthropology. I argue for bringing African cinemas out of the margins into the discipline of mainstream film studies and showcasing the diverse cinematic expressions of the continent. The decision to inscribe this book within a film studies framework should be understood as a desire to break away from what Moradewun Adejunmobi refers to as "the expansive position that textual interpretation occupies in studies of African cinema relative to other possible paths of research inquiry" (2016, 129). In this regard, beyond the textual interpretation mode of analysis, there is a need for, for instance, "analyses that take seriously the composition and editing of shots, along with soundtrack choices" (Brown, 2016, 144). The textbook heeds such calls by including three chapters on stylistic elements, namely African film music, cinematography, and animation, which still remain largely unexplored relative to their potential.

This second edition brings new materials and perspectives, profoundly different from the first edition. These are not cosmetic changes to existing chapters but rather adding new chapters to expand the scope and depth of the textbook. *African Film Studies: An Introduction* is organized around free-standing chapters, which are themselves grouped under five main parts: History of African Cinemas, Aesthetics in African Cinemas, African Film Criticism, Traditions and Practices in African Screen Media, and Notes on Streaming. Each chapter contains special features, including case studies, and suggested reading and screening lists to enable the reader to better expand their knowledge of African filmmaking practices and traditions. In Part I, the chapters on the history of African cinemas look at the film medium in Africa from colonial import and 'appropriation of the gaze' to the quest for individuality. They also establish parallels in the historical development of sub-Saharan African cinemas and African American cinema. In Part II, three chapters on aesthetics examine stylistic elements through cinematography, music, and animation. Part III, "African Film Criticism," presents an overview of selected critical reading lenses in scholarship on African cinemas. The newly added fourth part, "Traditions and Practices in African Screen Media," gathers chapters which seek not only to expand more geographical representation, but also to capture new directions of African screen media production and distribution. These chapters address Ethiopian cinema, Nollywood, and the production and distribution of African TV serials. The fifth and closing part on the streaming rush for Africa analyzes how the intervention of streaming companies in the African film and media landscape presents both opportunities and challenges for African creatives.

This edition of the textbook, as was the case with the first edition, rightly does not lay claim to comprehensiveness in capturing, in its entirety, the diversity of African cinematic practices and traditions across geographic and linguistic divides. Any attempt to render a comprehensive picture of African cinema(s) in a single book is bound to fall short of its well-intentioned ambitions. So, it is not my intention to oversimplify Africa's rich filmic corpus, nor to generalize the sociopolitical and economic conditions that shape production and distribution of African cinemas. Instead, I seek to provide teachers and undergraduate students an entry point into a cinema that still remains largely underexposed in the larger field of film and media studies despite its creative artistry and consistent output and prestigious prizes awarded to African films at international festivals.

Bibliography

Adejunmobi, Moradewun. "African Media Studies and Marginality at the Center." *Black Camera* 7, no. 2 (Spring 2016): 125–139.

Ashbury, Roy, Wendy Helsby, and Maureen O'Brien. *Teaching African Cinema.* London: British Film Institute, 1998.

Brown, H. Matthew. "African Screen Media Studies: Immediacy, Modernization, and Informal Forms." *Black Camera* 7, no. 2 (Spring 2016): 140–158.

Ellerson, Beti. "Teaching African Women in Cinema: Part Two." *Black Camera* 7, no. 2 (2016): 217–233.

Gugler, Josef. "African Films in the Classroom." *African Studies Review* 53, no. 3 (2010): 1–17.

1   What Is African Cinema?

What Is African Cinema?

African cinema(s) can be defined as a desire of freedom of African people to see themselves on screens through their own stories in locally sustainable film industries.[1] The definition encompasses a range of subject matter from the constricting structural and historical factors in production and distribution, audiences' relatability to and identification with on-screen stories, situating African productions in larger trends of increasingly new technology-driven circulation of content (streaming), and cinema as a business ecosystem of interactions between local stakeholders and the intervention of foreign companies. Obviously, there is no single and unifying definition of African cinema(s) for an artistically, culturally, and linguistically diverse continent. It is all about the perspective and critical reading lens from which the subject matter is examined. This definition provides a starting point for what African cinema is.

Let's start off with a snapshot of Africa's film industry with statistics to provide an overview of size, contribution to gross domestic product, and challenges, as indicated in data from the UNESCO-commissioned report *L'industrie du film en Afrique: tendances, défis et opportunités de croissance*[2] which was published in late 2021. The continent-wide, most comprehensive report in decades not only offers a complex and nuanced view of the current state of the film industry as of its publication but also prospectively examines the untapped growth potential. The film industry currently employs five million people and contributes $5 billion to Africa's gross domestic product (10). These numbers could quadruple, leading to $20 billion in yearly revenues and 20 million people employed. Unresolved questions remain, including what the best economic model is, streaming, structural challenges in production and distribution, persistence of gender inequality/inequity with actresses and female directors making up only between 10 and 30 percent of the industry (7), the

DOI: 10.4324/9781003246763-1

preservation and accessibility of copies of some of the old African films from the 1960s to the 1980s held by public and private organizations in the Global North,[3] and the impact of the COVID-19 pandemic in further exposing and accentuating existing structural deficiencies in distribution infrastructure and production practices.

Now moving on to the metadiscourse on what African cinema is, specifically the thematic treatment of the topic itself in African films, the opening scene of the film *Aristotle's Plot* (1996) by the Cameroonian director Jean-Pierre Bekolo is very insightful about the question. The film opens on a police officer and two handcuffed thug-looking individuals walking alongside rail tracks, with one dressed in black skin-tight leather pants and suit and the other wearing an unbuttoned coat that shows his naked chest and belly. The two handcuffed individuals are the filmmaker Essomba Tourneur, who was deported from Europe to his home country, and the gangster-movie enthusiast nicknamed 'Cinema.' At the rail track crossing, they make a sharp left turn and walk toward the camera before making a sudden stop by a parked police car. 'Cinema' bursts out laughing, and then asks the police officer, "Do you know that this is cinema?", in reference to the very scene of the three. The incredulous police officer replied with "what is cinema?" The ensuing discussion among the three characters centers on questions of whether cinema is acting out or a representation of reality and who can talk with authority about cinema: a director or a film enthusiast who has watched more than 10,000 films? The discussion occurs while moments earlier the voice-over narrator posed questions about the place of African cinema in the larger film history, as the British Film Institute had commissioned Jean-Pierre Bekolo to make a movie for the celebration of the centenary of cinema—*Aristotle's Plot*. The underlying idea of the opening scene is that of a metadiscourse[4] on cinema, but also most importantly of what African cinema is, which this chapter will attempt to answer.

The widely used term of 'African cinema' in scholarship often refers implicitly, unless explicitly specified to include North Africa, to all cinematic productions from sub-Saharan Africa regardless of the differences in the historical development of cinema traditions or linguistic and geographic differences that are evident in the diversity of productions. The use of such a generalizing/totalizing term to designate the entirety of continental productions is found almost nowhere in the world, as other productions are rarely addressed under the continental umbrella such as European, American, or Asian cinema. Instead, they are referred to through national frameworks such as, for instance, French, Italian, Japanese, US (Hollywood), Czech, or German cinema. The understanding and appreciation of African cinema(s) needs to depart from stereotypical perceptions of Africa as a monolithic entity in order to discern its richly textured artistic expressions. In addition to audiovisual productions, totalizing representations of the African continent are also evident in other mediums, as Wainaina Binyavanga's provocative essay "How to Write About Africa" demonstrates by detailing, in an ironic tone, recurrent clichés about black Africa that are found in literary forms and popular culture. The origins of these clichés can be traced back to what V. Y. Mudimbe (*The Invention of Africa*, 1988) refers to as the "invention of Africa" by the West, and to the scramble for Africa in the late 19th century by Europe, which has led to the division of the continent into territories controlled and exploited by colonial powers. During colonial times, film was used not only as entertainment for the mostly urban colonial settlers, but importantly as a pedagogical instrument to educate indigenous people to be become 'civilized.' To that end, the colonialized black subject is often stereotypically represented as a gullible buffoon and unsophisticated figure in films such as *Sanders of the River* (Zoltan Korda, 1935), *King Solomon's Mines* (Compton Bennett and Andrew Marton, 1950), *Le Grand blanc de Lambaréné* (*The Great White Man of Lambarene*, 1995) by Bassek ba Kobhio, and *Matamata and Pilipili* (Tristan Bourland, 1997).

The use of the collective term 'African cinema' may not necessarily be itself a completely wrong choice, but it has to be contextualized and understood within the framework of diverse cinematic traditions and practices on the continent. In this regard, we argue for the definition and understanding of Africa(ns) by taking into consideration the various iterations and traditions in moviemaking on the continent, including the colonial language divide (French, English, and Portuguese), the Sahara divide (north and south of the Sahara), art and celluloid French-speaking West African cinema, and the video and commercial Nollywood movies. Because "it would be far better if scholars could avoid regarding the continent as one, huge geographical landmass; otherwise we will continue to cover the space of Africa with blanket stereotypes" (Orlando, 2017, 11). Fortunately, there are a number of scholarly productions that approach African cinema in its pluralistic expressions: *African Filmmaking: Five Formations* (2017) by Kenneth Harrow, *Postcolonial African Cinema: Ten Directors* (2007) by David Murphy and Patrick Williams, *African Film: Re-Imagining a Continent* (2004) by Josef Gugler, and *African Filmmaking: North and South of the Sahara* (2006) by Roy Armes.

Diversity of the filmic corpus is not enough by itself to accurately and comprehensively provide a definition of African cinema(s) because other characteristic features will have to be explored to determine whether there are convergences and noticeable trends across the linguistic and geographic differences. In other words, what are the criteria by which to best assess the African-ness of films or their categorizations as belonging to African cinema(s): geography, language, genre, aesthetics, similar historical background in production and distribution, or content?

We believe that the reading lenses of content, aesthetics, and production and distribution offer insightful perspectives in defining African cinema(s) on its own, but also in establishing parallels with other cinematic traditions around the world. Content covers the ideological dimension of African film and the thematic treatment of issues relevant to the continent and its global positionality. As for the aesthetics, it concerns the development of Africa's cinematic grammar through stylistic elements such as orality, collective enunciation, and sociocultural beliefs. The dominant production and distribution patterns in Africa are those of an independent cinema existing outside the mainstream industry.

In certain cases, African cinema is defined by often underlining the ideological dimension of its films, hence the term of *cinema engagé*— politically committed—to refer to African directors who conceive of cinema as a medium whose main function is to educate, raise awareness, and liberate peoples from different forms of oppression and exploitation. For those directors, film is the most appropriate instrument to educate the majority of the African illiterate masses and to address the issue of controlling the narrative that is confronted by historically oppressed people. Film contributes not only to deconstruct and strike back at the colonial empire, in defining the narrative and representation of Africans by Africans for the rest of the world, but equally important to keep postcolonial African leadership accountable to the people. The ideological significance of African films is evident in a number of mechanisms[5] designed to further the appropriation of the medium as an instrument for political and cultural liberation at the inception of African cinema in the 1960s.

The Algiers Charter on African Cinema (1975) and the Niamey Manifesto of African Filmmakers (1982) were developed by the Pan-African Federation of Filmmakers (FEPACI) to help achieve political and cultural freedom from (neo)colonialism. Anticolonial rhetoric and critique of postcolonial African societies are the subject matter of films ranging from the art house films of francophone West Africa, the predominant documentary productions from Lusophone Africa to the post-apartheid South Africa's films by black directors exploring violence and reconciliation in the process of the rainbow nation building. Examples of such films include Sarah Maldoror's 1972 *Sambizanga*, Med Hondo's 1986 *Sarraounia*, Ousmane Sembène's 1988 *Camp de Thiaroye*, *The Great White Man of Lambarene* (1995) by Bassek ba Kobhio, and *Drum* (2004) by Zola

Maseko. In addition to the overtly politically committed films, there are social-issue movies such as Moustapha Alassane's 1972 *FVVA* on the devastating effects of consumerist behavior/economies at both the individual and social levels, *Yaaba* (1989) by Idrissa Ouédraogo on social exclusion in a rural setting, or Fanta Regina Nacro's 2004 *The Night of Truth* and Maria João Ganga's 2004 *Hollow City* on armed ethnic conflicts in Africa. While there is undoubtedly a corpus of political content in African film, this cannot be regarded as the most defining feature of African cinema because there is always an ideological dimension to any cultural production, be it African or not. In addition, the video-based technological innovation from the 1990s has led to a gradual shift from art house and intellectual cinema to a popular and commercial cinema in which political undertones are not always salient or not the focus of viewers. In this regard, Nigeria's video-based film industry—Nollywood—represents a different approach to film function as an educational tool in emphasizing entertainment over ideology. However, ideology and entertainment are not mutually exclusive, as it would also be a mistaken claim to suggest that all Nollywood productions are apolitical. Nollywood can be defined as a film industry, primarily based in southern Nigeria, that uses video technologies to revolutionize production, distribution, and reception of audiovisual stories—known in Africa and in the diaspora by different names such as home videos, home movies, or videofilms. These productions are mostly in Yoruba and/or English languages, as opposed to Kanywood, which are the Hausa-language productions from northern Nigeria. The commercial and popular success of this kind of video-based productions is evident in other countries such as Bongowood in Tanzania and Ghallywood in Ghana.

In addition to *cinema engagé*, African cinema could be defined based on thematic treatment, that is, how or whether film content reflects realities of the continent. Do movies adequately showcase the historical forces that shaped Africa's present and how its future could be conceptualized based on present-day challenges and opportunities? To what extent does thematic treatment showcase local imaginaries and stories in order to enable African viewership to appropriate and identify with on-screen images? According to the Tanzanian filmmaker, scholar, and former director of the Zanzibar International Film Festival, Martin Mhando, defining African cinema based on content "means seeing films as products of environmental and social conditions, historical pressures and technological innovations, as well as of the beliefs, attitudes, and cultural perceptions of the African people" (2014, 5). In this regard, African cinema could be regarded as a colonial imported medium that is appropriated by Africans to tell their stories from their own perspectives. For instance, topics such as Africa's past, historic figures, the encounter with the West, local sociocultural practices, and issues facing contemporary African societies contribute to the reception by and identification of spectators with audiovisual stories as their own. While the African-ness of film content may be considered as to how closely content portrays cultural and historical realities on the continent, it should however be noted that outside forces through transnational issues are increasingly shaping what would be referred to as intrinsically African. The treatment of global topics such as religious extremism, the environment, economic interconnectedness, and immigration has given rise to what Valérie K. Orlando refers to as "Afropolitan filmmaking" since the 2000s. Films such as *Little Senegal* (2001) by Rachid Bouchareb, Moussa Toure's 2004 *La Pirogue* (*The Pirogue*), *Pumzi* (2009) by Wanuri Kahiu, and *Timbuktu* (2014) by Abderrahmane Sissako bring to the fore questions concerning the global positionality of Africa and the intersections between Africa and the (black) world. The filmographies of the directors Abderrahmane Sissako, Rachid Bouchareb, and Andrew Dosunmu are particularly insightful as examples of work on the interactions between the continent and the rest of the world instead of focusing solely on an intrinsic African content.

Content is not only defined by 'what' is treated, but equally impactful is from 'whose' perspective is the story told. In other words, the gaze behind the gaze distorts content, or, better put, reveals more about the gaze holder than who is in front of the camera. Examples of gaze-tainted content are pervasive in film studies: portrayals of Africans in colonial cinema such as in *Sanders of the River* (Korda, 1935) and *Silvia the Zulu* (Gatti, 1928); and D.W. Griffith's depictions of African Americans in *The Birth of a Nation* (1915) as untrustworthy, morally dubious, sexually obsessed, and infantile figures. In addition, in her seminal article "Visual Pleasure and Narrative Cinema," Laura Mulvey demonstrates how on-screen representations of the female subject are informed by the male gaze behind the camera who projects his fantasies. The question of gaze is particularly relevant in the case of movies shot on location about Africa, with mostly non-African (black) movie stars, by Western directors. It is conceptually challenging to regard them as African movies, although they may reflect African historical and contemporary realities. Thematically, these movies fall into two categories: films made about the Rwandan genocide and movies inspired by historic and contemporary heroes such as Nelson Mandela's life and fight against apartheid. Examples include *Hotel Rwanda* (2004) by Terry George, featuring the African American actor Don Cheadle as the main protagonist, and *Sometimes in April* (2005) by the Haitian director Raoul Peck, Justin Chadwick's 2013 *Mandela: Long Walk to Freedom*, where Idris Elba plays

Nelson Mandela, and Clint Eastwood's 2009 *Invictus*, featuring Morgan Freeman as Nelson Mandela. The 2012 book *Hollywood's Africa After 1994*, edited by MaryEllen Higgins, provides further investigation into the interpretation of African stories by non-African filmmakers, which has a long practice dating back to the silent film era (Oscherwitz, 2012, 240–241). These films show how limiting the criterion of content can be, thus compelling us to broaden the understanding of African cinema to other parameters, including aesthetics in its formal elements (art).

African Cinema: Art or Business?

Filmmaking is an endeavor that blends artistry and moneymaking in different ways. Large funds must be raised in order to effectively produce a film and distribute it through several channels (theatrical release, online streaming, VOD, etc.). This is an industry that employs millions of people and generates billions of dollars every year worldwide. As a way of generating more revenue and profits, film studios or producers are keen to capitalize on the success of a particular movie by creating a franchise, remakes, or merchandising (movie-related products). Before coming on to the screens and maybe enjoying some commercial success, a movie is foremost a series of creative decisions in its developmental process where the director conveys his/her artistic vision. The director's creative choices, ranging from the selection of location, costume, actors' performance, and cinematography to special effects, will greatly shape the audience's experience of the movie. In certain cases, the business dimension drives the creative process, as in Hollywood cinema, while in other instances, artistic creativity is the primary focus of filmmaking, as is the case with experimental or avant-garde films. This book does not, however, consider art and business to be mutually exclusive. However, for African cinema, it will be important to examine the art and business dimensions in a way that sheds light on questions that might otherwise be overlooked. Is there a sustainable film industry in Africa? What are the film distribution networks in Africa at the national and transnational levels? Are there aesthetic features shared by several African films?

Art

Aesthetics in film is generally about how the subject matter or content is rendered or (re)presented through the director's creative vision. In this context, content and aesthetics are not generally treated separately, as it is the effective blending of the two that enhances the emotional or dramatic charge of a film. However, for the purpose and scope of the analysis of the artistic expressions in African cinema, the emphasis will be more on the 'how' (aesthetics) than the 'what' (content). Do African films share similar aesthetic features? In other words, are there any defining artistic traits of African cinema, selectively or globally? On these interrogations, the scholarship on African cinema falls into three categories, with an argument against authenticity,[6] a focus on the influence of oral cultures[7] on the narrative structures of several African films, and the transnational or Afropolitan trend[8] of African cinema. The objective here is not to take sides or try to essentialize African cinema, but to open an inquiry into whether there are some unifying creative features of African cinema, even if these features may either only apply to a particular corpus of films or be specific to certain directors. So, it should be understood that no claim is laid to the existence of a unique African film grammar or to one single shared aesthetics for the plurality of African productions. Instead, the focus is on two selected elements that can help highlight the artistic expressions in the case of West and Central African cinema: orality-inspired storytelling and the auteur cinema tradition.

Orality can be defined in the African sociocultural context as a knowledge production and transmission mechanism from one generation to the next. Collective knowledge is produced and disseminated through songs, short stories, tales, incantations, dance, and performances. The griot(te) is a central figure in the orality tradition as s/he is known to perform several functions as educator, counselor, negotiator, entertainer, and custodian of the collective memory. Mastery of the spoken word and possessing a profound knowledge of history are essential to the griot storytelling, an art that is passed down through family lines. Generally, one is born a griot, however, contemporary West African societies have witnessed reconfigurations of the griot through the emergence of popular musicians or entertainers (DJ Arafat, Debordo Leekunfa, Serge Beynaud, Claire Bahi, et al.). Several African films show similarities with the orality narrative structure or form in which stories are told as entertaining and didactic tales, facilitating local audiences' accessibility and identification with them. In this respect, the films of the internationally known Nigerian director Tunde Kelani showcase the hallmarks of popular forms of Yoruba culture and an inclination toward didacticism. In other instances, orality-inspired storytelling foregrounds important questions facing West African societies on identity, education, modernity, gender, and power. *Keïita! The Heritage of the Griot* (Dani Kouyaté, 1995) brings to the fore the questions of identity and education in a fast-changing society. The film's plot follows the initiation of the 6th grader Mabo into the meaning of his last name "Fofana" by Djeliba who came from the village. The film's narrative structure is built around the story of 15th-century Malian empire founder Sundjata. The modernist approach to traditions centered on the griot figure is also evident in *Djeli, conte d'aujourd'hui* (Fadika Kramo-Lanciné, 1981) where Kramoko, the son of a griot, cannot marry Fanta who is from a noble caste. As for *Taafe Fanga* (*Skirt Power*, 1997) by Adama Drabo, it opens on a griot proposing to tell an evening crowd about the story of women who once assumed the roles and responsibilities of men in their village. In these films or many of Ousmane Sembène's films, "the griot is shown performing various functions as actor/narrator" (Pfaff, 1993, 15). In addition to the griot figure, influence of different elements (tales, songs, incantations, initiatory journeys, and performances) of the oral cultures on West African cinema is also evident in productions such as *Xala* (Ousmane Sembène, 1974), *Yeelen* (Souleymane Cissé, 1987), and *Bal Poussière* (Dancing in the Dust, 1988) by Henri Duparc. Obviously, there is more to West African cinema than artistic constructions influenced by oral cultures; so this is not meant to be a reductionist presentation of the plurality of films.

The auteur cinema has a particularly longstanding tradition in francophone Africa because of a combination of different factors such as the influence of French New Wave (Ngangura, 1996, 62), and the funding and cooperation mechanisms set up by the French government to support film productions in francophone African countries (Barlet, 2012, 209; Hoefert de Turégano, 2002, 26–27). These mechanisms have also allowed continued French influence[9] on the aesthetic forms of African cinema. Auteur cinema is a practice or tradition where the director is regarded as an artist because s/he shows a unique style across productions. The director, whose artistic vision is the one viewers see on screen, is the creative force in filmmaking. In the African context, that auteur cinema tradition has taken the form of filmmakers being the one-man orchestra, performing the functions of producer, writer, director, editor, and publicist. As a result, actors do not always get as much media coverage and exposure as directors do. So, the local conditions of production and distribution, very similar to independent cinema, have also played an important role in presenting the director as the cornerstone of filmmaking. In this kind of auteur/independent cinema, commercial viability did not always appear to drive filmmaking, as productions were usually funded by state, bilateral (French Ministry of Foreign Affairs), or multilateral institutions (European Union and Francophonie). This is particularly true for the first and second generations of African filmmakers such as Ousmane Sembène, Med Hondo, Oumarou Ganda, Moustapha Alassane, Souleymane Cissé, Djibril Diop Mambéty, Gaston Kaboré, and Idrissa Ouédraogo. Some of these directors have developed their unique styles of filmmaking or storytelling, which is manifested through their works.

As one of the pioneers of African cinema, Sembène's work is distinguishable by the sociorealist representation of the quotidian, anticolonial rhetoric, the thematic treatment of women's empowerment, and a critique of postcolonial elites. For Françoise Pfaff, "the originality of Ousmane Sembène as a filmmaker lies in having managed successfully to adapt film, a primarily Western medium, to the needs, pace, and rhythm of African culture" (1993, 13). Concerning Souleymane Cissé, his films are mostly constructed around a social critique paradigm, with *Yeelen* standing out as a highly political masterpiece that showcases creative aesthetics (see the case study on *Yeelen* vs. *Daughters of the Dust* in Chapter 3). The need to bring about sociopolitical changes has led some African filmmakers like Sembène and Cissé, according to James E. Genova, "to explore Soviet cinematographic traditions or to seek inspiration from other disruptive cinematic styles like Italian neorealism, Latin American cinema novo, and Third Cinema" (2013, 15). For his unconventional and original storytelling, Djibril Diop Mambéty is highly regarded as a director who seeks to reinvent cinema, particularly his first feature-length film, *Touki Bouki* (1973), and second feature, *Hyenas* (1992). This particular focus on form is prolonged in the works of certain filmmakers of the later generation, especially Jean-Pierre Bekolo and John Akomfrah. For instance, Bekolo advocates for African cinema to develop its unique language that draws on local realities, thus contributing its creativity to the cinematic medium at large. He places great emphasis on innovative form as a key component to filmmaking by rejecting formulaic repetition of forms as a practice of creation—mimesis. Cinema, for Bekolo, means a constant reinvention by going beyond established norms of storytelling and aesthetics to create or enhance ways of treating a subject matter. It should, however, be noted that auteur cinema is currently going through different reconfigurations because of the scarcity of state and institutional funding sources that have traditionally supported this kind of cinema. In addition to auteur cinema, which tends be distributed through art house cinema theaters in the West, filmmakers need now to produce commercial entertainment films to generate revenue for their next projects. But these two orientations are not mutually exclusive, at least for Bekolo. Popular entertainment and the search for creative aesthetics are the hallmarks of Bekolo's films (*Quartier Mozart* in 1992, *Aristotle's Plot* in 1996, and his 2005 *Les saignantes* [The Bloodettes]), which Akin Adesokan refers to as "aesthetic populism" (2008, 4). Kunle Afolayan's *The Figurine* (2009) also demonstrates that Nollywood commercial films are not incompatible with artistic creativity, considering the often-justified criticism leveled at the poor quality of movies from the beginnings of Nollywood.

Business

In terms of annual output, "Nollywood is now widely acknowledged as the third largest film industry in the world, after the United States (Hollywood) and India (Bollywood)" (Adesokan, 2011, 81). It generates millions of dollars in revenue for the local economy. Similarly, the South African film industry has grown from R20 million a year at the end of apartheid to R5.4 billion by March 2018.[10] The film industries in these two sub-Saharan countries are performing well. But what is the current situation of the overall African film industry? To answer this question, it is important to examine African cinema through four essential elements that shape the formation and operation of a film industry: distribution, organization, human capital (professionals), and the audience. Distribution generally involves considerable investment in the physical infrastructure (movie theaters), and now the circulation of images occurs through online platforms as digital technologies are changing delivery modes and consumption patterns. The closing of movie theaters over the past two decades in sub-Saharan countries, as a consequence of the IMF-imposed Structural Adjustment Programs (SAPs)[11] in the 1990s, has left theatrical distribution in a relatively bad situation. However, the governments of Burkina Faso, Côte d'Ivoire, and Senegal have developed different initiatives since the 2000s to either rehabilitate old theaters or build new ones. From private businesses, the French conglomerate Bolloré has already built a number of Canal Olympia theaters in several capital cities in francophone African countries, with more planned constructions of multifunctional high-tech theaters. While streaming services are not fully developed to their potential on the continent, the televisual channel of distribution allows for transnational flows of images, especially through the transitional media corporations and satellite television companies such as M-Net (Africa Magic), Africable, Canal+ and its African subsidiary A+, and TV5MONDE Afrique. They distribute African content such as films and an ever-increasing number of TV series. The festival circuit also offers media and film professionals business meeting opportunities like the Marché International du Cinéma et de la Télévision Africains (MICA) during FESPACO editions to buy and sell films or TV productions. Studio filmmaking is yet to be widely developed on the continent, with local films mostly shot on location. The Moroccan city of Ouarzazate is well known internationally for hosting some of the most successful Hollywood productions such as *Gladiator,*

Lawrence of Arabia, and *Game of Thrones*. In the early 1980s, private African businesspeople have created movie studios with mixed results. Martial Ouédraogo founded Cinafric in 1981 only to be closed a few years later (Diawara, 1992, 76). As for The Atlas Film Studio founded in 1983 by the Moroccan entrepreneur Mohamed Belghmi, it has had better success than Ouédraogo's. Today, more privately owned film production companies are still being considered such as the Ghallywood studio project by the Ghanaian producer William Akuffo (Garritano, 2013, 12), and the Burkinabe actor Hippolyte Ouangrawa's current project to build Laadowood Studio, 50 kilometers outside Ouagadougou on land of 10 acres, especially for comedy productions. Ouangrawa is a very popular comedian who has played in many Burkinabe comedy TV series and feature films.

The way film business activities are organized and conducted provides great insights into the market as to whether it is self-regulated, government-regulated, a vertical integration of its different entities, or an informally operated system. A first look at the landscape of film industry shows a disparate picture across geographical areas or countries with regard to the level of organization and development. North Africa and South Africa appear to have far better formally organized film industries, while some West African countries such as Burkina Faso, Ghana, Côte d'Ivoire, and Senegal have recently either passed laws or created film funds designed to contribute to the emergence of national cultural industries, particularly cinema. Overall, the African film industry will need more structuring and streamlining to enable fluid business interactions from producers and directors to exhibitors as is the case in the West. For instance, few countries currently have in place a box office system, which could provide reliable and timely data to assess the performance of local new releases. In the wider context of the film industry globally, profound systemic changes are happening: movies are being released simultaneously on streaming platforms and in theaters; there is a shortened time frame between theatrical release and VOD; and for many Netflix films and original series there is only streaming.

Concerning human capital, there are quality professionals to fill different positions in the industry: producers, writers, directors, actors, and technicians (camera, sound, and editing). The numerous film schools open in certain African countries (Burkina Faso, Senegal, Gabon, Kenya, South Africa, Morocco, et al.) provide training and a steady supply of technicians that the African film industry will need for its development. In addition to film schools to train technicians, there should also be more acting schools created across the continent to foster the emergence and growth of a larger pool of talent. More importantly, the status of actors is precarious, because of the absence of legal or institutional frameworks at national levels to regulate their profession with regard to their status, pay rate, and working conditions. One option for them could be to be unionized or to organize themselves into professional organizations like the Actors Guild of Nigeria, for instance. For the directors, there is the Nairobi-based Pan-African Federation of Filmmakers (FEPACI), which is a professional body of representation, advocacy, and networking.

For any film industry to thrive, it is imperative to have an audience. In underlining the distribution challenges facing African cinema, namely audiences on the continent not readily having access to African films, Olivier Barlet portrays African cinema as "an audience without a market" (2010, 81). However, what is undeniably true is the fact that there is a public for African cinema both on the continent and in the diaspora. The public's enthusiasm to see African movies playing in local theaters, the innumerable number of pirated movie copies circulating online or on DVD, and the popularity of locally made TV series all attest to the existence of an audience for African audiovisual content.

Accessibility: Where to Find African Films?

The question of film availability is important for both teachers preparing a new course and students seeking additional information before enrolling in a film course, particularly if certain films are scheduled on the syllabus as outside-of-class viewing assignments. The accessibility question is even more poignant for African film, as a form of minor cinema, within the global context of mainstream cinema distribution. What resources are available to help locate African film titles or to keep abreast of new releases? How to acquire or watch these films? In response to these interrogations, here are some resources that are not meant to be exhaustive but to guide teachers and students:

- **Online Streaming Platforms**: Amazon video, Netflix, YouTube, Kanopy, Hulu, iROKOtv
- **Independent Film Distributors (DVDs)**: ArtMattan, Kino Lorber, California Newsreel, Women Make Movies, Icarus, Documentary Educational Resources, Médiathèque des Trois Mondes, FNAC, and Editions Montparnasse
- **Institutional Resources**: public libraries, the global network of Institut Français and French cultural centers, interlibrary loans (US-based universities and colleges), and museums
- **Informal Circuits**: street vendors and African stores in major US and European cities

- **Festival Circuit**:
  Journées Cinématographiques de Carthage (Tunisia)
  FESPACO: Pan-African Film and Television Festival of
      Ouagadougou (Burkina Faso)
  Écrans Noirs (Cameroon)
  Durban International Film Festival (South Africa)
  Zanzibar International Film Festival (Tanzania)
  Ciné Droit Libre (human rights film festival in Burkina Faso, Senegal,
      Côte d'Ivoire, and Mali)
  i-Represent International Film Festival (Nigeria)
  Lagos International Festival of Animation (Nigeria)
  Abuja International Film Festival (Nigeria)
  Rencontres du Film Court (Madagascar)
  New York African Film Festival (USA)
  Harlem African Animation Festival
  African Diaspora International Film Festival (USA)
  New Voices in Black Cinema (USA)
  Brooklyn Academy of Music (USA)
  Vues d'Afrique (Canada)
  Locarno Festival (Switzerland)
  Festival Cinémas d'Afrique (Switzerland)
  Film Africa (England)
  Africa in Motion Film Festival (Scotland)
  Cambridge African Film Festival (England)
  Festival Cinema Africano, Asia e America Latina (Italy)
- **African Film Database**:
  The Black Film Center/Archive (Indiana University)
  La cinémathèque française (Paris, France)
  La cinémathèque africaine de Ouagadougou (Burkina Faso)
  www.afrique.tv5monde.com (under VIDÉOS tab)
  www.africanfilmdatabase.com
  www.colonialfilm.org.uk
- **How to stay updated on the latest news on African cinema:**
  www.africultures.com (and its weekly newsletter *Africultures*)
  www.africine.org (African Federation of Film Critics)
  www.indiewire.com (numerous articles on African cinema)
  www.fespaco.bf/en/ (FESPACO)
  www.facebook.com/AfricanFilmTalkSeries/ ("African Cinema
      Talk Series" on Facebook and YouTube by Boukary Sawadogo)
  www.africanwomenincinema.blogspot.com (Beti Ellerson)
  www.fepacisecretariat.org (Pan-African Federation of Filmmakers)
  www.cinemaescapist.com

Case Study: *Aristotle's Plot* (Jean-Pierre Bekolo, 1996)

Aristotle's Plot was commissioned by the British Film Institute for its "Centenary of Cinema" series and is a metadiscourse on the definition of cinema, particularly African cinema. The film's plot is constructed around a disenchanted African director and a group of die-hard movie enthusiasts who disagree over what (African) cinema is. The director, Essomba Tourneur, has been deported to his home country and struggles to reintegrate into a world in which "stories have replaced reality." He crosses paths with a group of gangsters infatuated with Hollywood cinema and living in the local movie theater, "Cinema Africa." Essomba has to face off with the gangsters after they steal his film reels that he brought back from Europe.

What Is Cinema?

The film's subplots—the police investigation, the question of what is cinema, the venues, the characters' identities, and their inner motives—are all connected to an interrogation that remains unresolved at the end of the movie. But it does not appear that Jean-Pierre Bekolo's primary goal is to give a complete definition of cinema, but rather to (re)introduce to the African audience certain basic questions about the film medium, such as the relationship between imagination and reality, how much of filmmaking is about technology, and the act of creation as a repetition of creative forms—mimesis. In this respect, the opening and closing scenes of the film are meant to immerse the viewer in the experience of a movie shoot. For instance, after Tourneur is run over by a car in the closing scene, he is walking toward the camera with his intestines hanging out. The gruesome injury and graphic nature of the scene are in stark contrast with his ability to walk, had this accident happened to him in real life. As Tourneur gets closer to the camera, the medium shot pulls wider, showing an unattended camera on a tripod. Then we hear the voice-over sarcastically noting that the camera operator should not leave his post because this is a real film shoot.

The demystification or deconstruction of filmmaking around the thematic treatment of reality versus fiction is evident in other African films, such as the short film *Un certain matin* (*A Certain Morning*, 1992) by Fanta Régina Nacro; and by on-screen characters enacting their dreams to be movie actors, such as the Sheriff character in *Ouaga Saga* (Dani Kouyaté, 2004) and the bored gangsters in *Aristotle's Plot* who are seeking "real action" like what they see in movies. The voice-over observation sounds like a warning: "The life of the gangsters has become an imitation of ignoble actions. Instead of imitating life, they are imitating an imitation of life" (43:00).

The larger framework beyond reality versus fiction concerns the driving force behind artistic creation: Is it imitation (mimesis) or deviation from established codes or norms? The Senegalese director Djibril Diop Mambéty prefers to keep the freshness and magic of the film medium, so he uses nonprofessional actors and never uses the same actors in two different movies (Ukadike, 2002, 128). Jean-Pierre Bekolo and Djibril Diop Mambéty (*Touki Bouki*, 1973; *Hyenas*, 1992) openly advocate for and consistently strive to develop new creative forms (from established patterns) across many films. *Yeelen* (1987), by Souleymane Cissé, develops some unique aesthetics in African cinema, as described in the case study in Chapter 3. But such groundbreaking storytelling is not demonstrated in any other film by Souleymane Cissé to the same extent as in *Yeelen*.

What Is African Cinema?

Do we define African cinema in relation to the larger film medium or by focusing on its characteristic traits in terms of production and distribution? In locating African cinema within the historical development trajectory of cinema, African cinema[12] may appear relatively young and disadvantaged because of its late start (in the 1960s) compared with cinema in the West, as alluded to in the voice-over in the opening sequence of *Aristotle's Plot*. So, how would Jean-Pierre Bekolo measure up to directors such as Jean-Luc Godard and Martin Scorsese in making the British Film Institute-commissioned films for the "Centenary of Cinema" series?

There is no correlation between the relatively young age of African cinema and the artistry of its filmmakers. African directors and actors have won prizes at FESPACO, Journées Cinématographiques de Carthage, the Cannes Film Festival, the Berlin International Film Festival, the British Academy of Film and Television Arts (BAFTA), and America's Academy Awards. In relation to mainstream commercial cinema, dominated by Hollywood, African cinema may be regarded as minor cinema in terms of production values and distribution, which are often similar to those of independent cinema.

In the specific context of African cinema, *Aristotle's Plot* addresses different questions of aesthetics, conditions of production and distribution, and the situation of the filmmaker. Compared with Hollywood productions, African films are often considered slow-paced, which is evident in how the gang leader, 'Cinema,' expresses his frustration while watching an African film: "These movies, you go out, take a piss, have a meal, they're still doing the same thing they're doing when you come back" (39:50).

This gross exaggeration may also be read as a caution against making generalizations, not only because different cinematic traditions around the world develop their own practices and ways of storytelling, but also because African cinema contains genre films (drama, thriller, action, and sci-fi) that are usually associated with fast-paced productions. We should also remember that the perceived pace or rhythm of a film, that is, how quickly the story is unfolding, includes parameters such as narration[13] and editing.[14] So, not all African films are slow.

The challenges of African film distribution, in the process of building a sustainable film industry, are raised in *Aristotle's Plot* by depicting alienated African viewers and disenfranchised filmmakers. The programming of the local movie theater is dominated by Hollywood productions, as the gangsters seem to have very good knowledge of Hollywood films but almost none about their own country's productions. This stems from the dominant position of Hollywood in theatrical distribution. As a result, the character of Essomba Tourneur, which epitomizes the condition of African filmmakers, is reduced to pushing his film reels in a cart around the city to search for a screening venue. Tourneur failed to make a film career in Europe and was deported to his home country, where he is also treated as a pariah and often ridiculed as a "silly ass" (in a play on the term "cineaste"). In his displacement, Essomba Tourneur—"Tourneur" means in French one who is constantly making loops—portrays the dilemma of African auteur directors whose films circulate mostly within the festival circuit while remaining inaccessible to mainstream African audiences. This practice is referred to as "calabash cinema."

Today, however, theatrical distribution is only one of several options available to audiovisual producers in Africa. Content delivery and consumption are gradually shifting to online platforms and portable electronic devices. Satellite and cable television channels such as M-Net, Africable, TV5MONDE Afrique, A+, and private TV stations operating locally in many countries are also helping alleviate the structural challenges in African film distribution.

For an understanding of African cinema based on production and distribution, Allison McGuffie puts African cinema into three categories:

- globally circulating, independent art-style cinema;
- audience-supported national and regional popular entertainment video-film industries; and
- developmental or educational cinema produced by the international humanitarian aid community (2015, 31).

These categorizations underline the multiple means of circulation for contemporary African cinema.

The question "quel cinéma africain?" ("African cinema?" 1975, 342) by the Senegalese film historian and critic, Paulin Soumanou Vieyra, in his seminal book *Le cinéma africain: des origines à 1973*, reflects the challenges faced by the first generation of African filmmakers. What cinema to make: Hollywood-style commercial cinema, develop a unique cinematic voice outside the mainstream, or a combination of commercial and auteur cinema? Five decades after the birth of postcolonial African cinema, all these questions are present in the productions made on the continent and in the diaspora. The global flow of images, the impact of digital technologies on film production and distribution, and the appropriation of 'globality' by African filmmakers[15] will have a significant bearing, for the foreseeable future, on defining African cinema and its orientations.

Notes

1 The definition drew on discussions of the webinar "Decolonizing African Cinema: Continuity and Change," hosted by the Sharjah (United Arab Emirates)-based Africa Institute on November 19, 2021. The Congolese filmmaker Balufu Bakupa Kanyinda and I were the two discussants of the webinar.

2 UNESCO, *L'industrie du film en Afrique: tendances, défis et opportunités de croissance* [*The African Film Industry: Trends, Challenges and Opportunities for Growth*], 2021.

3 Public discourse on the restitution of African films has gained much more attention since early 2022, following the battle for African artifacts to be returned to the continent. Funding is the major mechanism through which Western production and distribution companies exert control over exhibition rights, copyrights, or ownership.

4 Self-reflective discussion of a particular subject matter: a discussion of cinema by cinema.

5 Similar manifestos such as the political and aesthetic movement, Third Cinema, founded by Octavio Getino and Fernando Solanas were developed in Latin America in the 1960s and 1970s to provide a counter-model to Hollywood.

6 David Murphy, Stephen A. Zacks, and Kenneth Harrow.

7 Manthia Diawara, Martin Mhando, Keyan G. Thomaselli, Arnold Shepperson, and Maureen Eke.

8 Sarah Hamblin, Suzanne Gauch, and Carmela Garritano.

9 Besides the French influence, African cinema manifests influences from Italian neorealism and Russian formalism through the training or ideological leanings of certain African directors.

10 These figures are from the National Film and Video Foundation (NFVF) and Brand South Africa (BSA).

11 SAP disrupted the burgeoning film industries in many countries such as Burkina Faso, Benin, Senegal, and Tanzania, which had nationalized film distribution in the 1970s to foster the emergence of national cinema. Ironically, SAP has been a catalyst to the emergence of Nollywood.

12 As opposed to cinema under colonial rule, postcolonial African cinema refers to when Africans took possession of the film medium.
13 How much information is withheld from the viewer and for how long.
14 Shot lengths and transitions between shots.
15 Several African filmmakers regularly work and live in at least two different countries.

Bibliography and Filmography

Adesokan, Akin. *Postcolonial Artists and Global Aesthetics*. Bloomington: Indiana University Press, 2011.

Adesokan, Akin. "The Challenges of Aesthetic Populism: An Interview with Jean-Pierre Bekolo." *Postcolonial Text* 4, no. 1 (2008): 1–11.

Barlet, Olivier. "African Filmmakers' New Strategies; From Métis to Nomadic; Cinema: An Audience without a Market; Five Decades of African Film." *Black Camera* 1, no. 2 (Summer 2010): 63–102.

Barlet, Olivier. "The Ambivalence of French Funding." *Black Camera* 3, no. 2 (2012): 205–216.

Binyavanga, Wainaina. "How to Write About Africa." *Granta* 92 (Winter 2005): 91–95.

Camp de Thiaroye. Dir. Ousmane Sembène. New Yorker Video, 1998.

Diawara, Manthia. *African Cinema: Politics and Culture*. Bloomington: Indiana University Press, 1992.

Diawara, Manthia. "Popular Culture and Oral Traditions in African Film." *Film Quarterly* 41, no. 3 (Spring 1988): 6–14.

Femme Villa Voiture Argent (FVVA). Dir. Moustapha Alassane. Martfilmes, 1972.

Garritano, Carmela. *African Video Movies and Global Desires: A Ghanaian History*. Athens: Ohio University Press and Swallow Press, 2013.

Gauch, Suzanne. *Maghrebs in Motion: North African Cinema in Nine Movements*. New York: Oxford University Press, 2016.

Genova, James E. *Cinema and Development in West Africa*. Bloomington and Indianapolis: Indiana University Press, 2013.

Hamblin, Sarah. "Toward a Transnational African Cinema: Image and Authenticity in La Vie sur terre." *Black Camera* 3, no. 2 (Spring 2012): 8–30.

Higgins, MaryEllen, ed. *Hollywood's Africa after 1994*. Athens: Ohio University Press, 2012.

Hoefert de Turégano, Teresa. "The New Politics of African Cinema at the French Ministry of Foreign Affairs." *French Politics, Culture & Society* 20, no. 3 (2002): 22–32.

Le Grand blanc de Lambaréné (The Great White Man of Lambarene). Dir. Bassek Ba Kobhio. California Newsreel, 1995.

Matamata and Pilipili. Dir. Tristan Bourland. Icarus Films, 1997.

McGuffie, Allison. "What is African Cinema? The Industries of African Cinema." In *Directory of World Cinema: Africa*, ed. Blandine Stefanson, and Sheila Petty, 31–35. Bristol and Chicago: Intellect Books and University of Chicago Press, 2015.

Mhando, Martin. "Approaches to African Cinema Study: Defining Other Boundaries." In *Critical Approaches to African Cinema Discourse*, ed. Frank Nwachukwu Ukadike, 3–22. Lanham and Plymouth: Lexington Books, 2014.

Moore, Cornelius. "African Cinema in the American Video Market." *Issue: A Journal of Opinion* 20, no. 2 (Summer 1992): 38–41.

Moore, Cornelius. "US Distribution of African Film: California Newsreel's Library of African Cinema: A Case Study." In *Viewing African Cinema in the Twentieth-First Century: Art Films and the Nollywood Video Revolution*, ed. Mahir Şaul and Ralph A. Austen, 225–230. Athens: Ohio University Press, 2010.

Mulvey, Laura. "Visual Pleasure and Narrative Cinema." In *Film Theory and Criticism: Introductory Readings*, ed. Leo Braudy and Marshall Cohen, 833–844. New York: Oxford University Press, 1999.

Ngangura, Dieudonné Mweze. "African Cinema: Militancy or Entertainment?" In *African Experiences of Cinema*, ed. Imruh Bakari and Mbaye Cham, 60–64. London: British Film Institute, 1996.

Night of the Truth. Dir. Fanta Regina Nacro. Global Lens, 2004.

Orlando, K. Valérie. *New African Cinema*. New Brunswick: Rutgers University Press, 2017.

Oscherwitz, Dayna. "Bye Bye Hollywood: African Cinema and its Double in Mahamet-Saleh Haroun's Bye Bye Africa." In *Hollywood's Africa after 1994*, ed. MaryEllen Higgins, 240–259. Athens: Ohio University Press, 2012.

Pfaff, Françoise. "The Uniqueness of Ousmane Sembene's Cinema." *Contributions in Black Studies* 11, no. 3 (1993): 13–19.

Sarraounia. Dir. Med Hondo. Statens Filmcentral, 1996.

Siliva the Zulu. Dir. Attilia Gatti and Giuseppe Vitrotti. Explorator Film, 1928.

The Birth of a Nation. Dir. D. W. Griffith. Kino on Video, 2002.

The Great White Man of Lambarene. Dir. Bassek Ba Kobhio. California Newsreel, 1995.

Tomaselli, G. Keyan, Arnold Shepperson, and Maureen Eke. "Towards a Theory of Orality in African Cinema." *Research in African Literatures* 26, no. 3 (1995): 18–35.

Ukadike, Frank Nwachukwu, ed. *Critical Approaches to African Cinema Discourse*. Lanham and Plymouth: Lexington Books, 2014.

Ukadike, Frank Nwachukwu, ed. *Questioning African Cinema: Conversations with Filmmakers*. Minneapolis: University of Minnesota Press, 2002.

United Nations Educational, Scientific and Cultural Organization. *The African Film Industry: Trends, Challenges and Opportunities for Growth*. Paris: UNESCO, 2021.

Vieyra, Paulin Soumanou. *Le cinéma africain: des origines à 1973*. Paris: Présence africaine, 1975.

Yaaba. Dir. Idrissa Ouédraogo. Médiathèque des trois mondes, 1989.

Zacks, Stephen A. "The Theoretical Construction of African Cinema." *Research in African Literatures* 26, no. 3 (1995): 6–17.

Suggested Readings and Films

Adesanmi, Puis. *You Are Not a Country, Africa*. Cape Town: Penguin Books, 2011.

Aristotle's Plot. Dir. Jean-Pierre Bekolo. AfricAvenir International, 1996.

Armes, Roy. *Dictionary of African Filmmakers*. Bloomington: Indiana University Press, 2008.

Bisschoff, Lizelle, and Ann Overbergh. "Digital as the New Popular in African Cinema? Case Studies from the Continent." *Research in African Literatures* 43, no. 4 (Winter 2012): 112–127.

Dovey, Lindiwe. *Curating Africa in the Age of Film Festivals*. New York: Palgrave Macmillan, 2015.

The Figurine. Dir. Kunle Afolayan. Golden Effects, 2009.

Givanni, June, ed. *Symbolic Narratives/African Cinema: Audiences, Theory and the Moving Image*. London: BFI Publishing, 2000.

Gugler, Josef. *African Film: Re-Imagining a Continent*. Bloomington: Indiana University Press, 2003.

Haffner, Pierre. *Essai sur les fondements du cinéma africain*. Dakar, Senegal: Nouvelles Éditions Africaines, 1978.

Harrow, W. Kenneth, and Carmela Garritano, eds. *A Companion to African Cinema*. Hoboken: Wiley Blackwell, 2019.

Harrow, W. Kenneth. *African Filmmaking: Five Formations*. East Lansing: Michigan State University Press, 2017.

Moore, Cornelius. "U.S. Distribution of African Film: California Newsreel's Library of African Cinema: A Case Study." In *Viewing African Cinema in the Twenty-First Century: Art Films and the Nollywood Video Revolution*, ed. Mahir Şaul and Ralph A. Austen, 225–230. Athens: Ohio University Press, 2010.

Mudimbe, V. Y. *The Invention of Africa*. Bloomington and Indianapolis: Indiana University Press, 1988.

Murphy, David, and Patrick Williams. *Postcolonial African Cinema: Ten Directors*. Manchester: Manchester University Press, 2007.

Orlando, Valérie K. *New African Cinema*. New Brunswick: Rutgers University Press, 2017.

Sippy, Priya. "As Africa's Artifacts Start to Be Returned, What About Its Films?" *Quartz Africa*, December 16, 2021. https://qz.com/africa/2103081/africas-restitution-debate-should-include-films/.

Solanas, Fernando, and Octavio Getino. "Toward a Third Cinema." *Cinéaste* 4, no. 3 (1970–1971): 1–10.

Stefanson, Blandine, and Sheila Petty, eds. *Directory of World Cinema: Africa*. Bristol and Chicago: Intellect Books and University of Chicago Press, 2015.

Thackway, Melissa. *Africa Shoots Back: Alternative Perspectives in Sub-Saharan Francophone Film*. Oxford: James Currey, 2003.

UNESCO. *The African Film Industry: Trends, Challenges and Opportunities for Growth*. Paris: UNESCO, 2021.

Welcome to Nollywood. Dir. Jamie Meltzer. Indiepix, 2007.

Part I
History of African Cinemas

2   History of African Cinemas

The chapter articulates two main dimensions of the history of the developmental trajectory of the film medium in Africa, including the African experience of cinema during colonial rule and the birth and development of a postcolonial African cinema since the 1960s.

Matamata and Pilipili (Tristan Bourlard, 1997) is a documentary that provides great insight into the history of cinema in Africa and the on-screen depiction of indigenous people under colonial rule. The *Matamata and Pilipili* comic series was made in the 1940s by the Belgian Reverend Father Albert Van Haelst as part of the church work in the region of Kasai (present-day Democratic Republic of Congo, DRC) to educate the masses. According to the documentary, Van Haelst made 150 films from the 1940s to 1960 until the independence of then Zaïre, 20 of which are the *Matamata Pilipili* comic series. The latter featured an African comedian duo made of the short and fat character of Matamata and the slender and smart figure of Pilipili. Built around mostly extensive excerpts of the *Matamata Pilipili* comic series, the documentary also includes interviews of Congolese people and retired priests who had served in DRC during the time of Van Haelst. The comic series, through a diverse thematic treatment, promotes assimilation to French culture and the virtues of the Christian faith. In its stereotypical representation of Africans through the characters of Matamata and Pilipili, the comic series reveals the gaze behind the camera—that is, a European gaze that reflects their own simplistic construction of Africa rather than the reality of a complex and rich continent. Nowhere is this more prominent than in the opening scene of the documentary with a medium shot of smiling Matamata, which is cut to a blackface—accentuating what is regarded as characteristic features of black people such as big lips, big noses, and laughing eyes. Then, the shot cuts to barefoot children in the street who are laughing at Matamata's performance, which the voice-over narrator lauds as that of a magician (0:0:11). The infantilization of Africans and moralistic overtones of the

DOI: 10.4324/9781003246763-3

narrative pervade the various comic episodes shown in the documentary. In addition, the fact that the names of Matamata and Pilipili were never listed in the opening or end credits of the comic series shows the complete disregard for their creative contribution to Van Haelst's cinematic productions. What the opening scene shows to the viewer is the stereotypical representation of the continent in moving image arts and the world's lack of knowledge of Africa, which is underlined by the generalization of its people and culture. Africa still remains on the margins in the study and teaching of the global history of film. It is high time we centered Africa in the process of writing and reading the global history of moving image arts. Little attention is often given to the place and role of Africa in the global history of cinema.

It is the aim of this chapter to ground the study of African film history within the context of cultural expressions that rose in response to the dominant discourse to help Africans forge their own identity and represent their *imaginaire collectif*.[1] Adopting such a critical lens to read African film history is certainly a challenging task because criticisms could be leveled at the risks of ghettoizing African cinema or the perception of a cinema that is fossilized in identity politics and militancy. However, these potential risks are outweighed by the appropriateness of an approach that will best underline "the social contexts in which the film narratives were produced and meant to be received" (Genova, 2013, 10). The historical origins of the film medium in Africa are closely connected to colonialism, which used film as a propaganda instrument for twofold objectives. Certain colonial propaganda films targeted indigenous populations to showcase the merits of the advanced civilization, while some were designed to rally more support at home for the colonial enterprise, particularly at a time when dissenting voices were being heard in Europe in the post-World War II context. This chapter chronologically and thematically examines African film history through three critical time periods: cinema under colonial rule before the 1960s, the pioneers and second generation of filmmakers from the 1960s to the 1980s, and the 1990s, when technological innovation set new trends in African filmmaking.

Africa under Colonial Rule: Cinema as an Instrument of the Empire

The first film screenings on the continent came relatively soon after the Lumière brothers' first public screening at the Grand Café in Paris on December 28, 1895, which is regarded as the first public movie screening in the history of cinema. "The first screenings in Africa of Lumière's

'Cinématographe' took place in Cairo and Alexandria as early as 1896," followed by Senegal in 1900, and Nigeria in 1903 (Ashbury et al., 1998, 39). The early introduction of cinema to other parts of Africa is well documented; James Burns notes that "Southern Africa's cinema history began in the late 19th century, when a travelling magician named Carl Hertz brought movies to the South African Republic as part of his act" (2015, 11). Despite contact with film in its early years, sub-Saharan Africa would exert little control over stories told about the continent. In other words, Africa's own constructed images are absent in the global flow of images that represent the continent to the rest of the world.

From the late 19th century to the 1960s, the production and distribution of motion pictures were tightly controlled by the colonial apparatus through a number of institutional and legal mechanisms throughout sub-Saharan Africa. Such mechanisms included "the British anthropological film programs of the Bantu Educational Kinema Experiment or the Colonial Film Unit" (Genova, 2013, 22), and the Laval Decree of 1934 that sought "through censorship to control the distribution, content, and audiences of films" in French colonies in Africa (Genova, 2013, 27). These initiatives were set up as prolongations of Western cultural domination, which further alienated the colonized from the construction of their own narrative. Consequently, this has meant for Africans what is referred to as "l'absence de notre image dans le mirroir"[2] by Balufu Bakupa-Kanyinda, the Congolese filmmaker and president of the African Guild of Directors. He advocates for the decolonization of the minds of African people in order to develop the continent, and the creation of sustainable cultural industries (cinema) that will contribute economic development and awareness raising. In this respect, there are similarities with Fanon's psychoanalytic approach to how the colonized subject needs to liberate his/her mind.

However, it should also be noted that the Colonial Film Units in British colonies and similar projects in territories under French rule provided the initial infrastructure and framework from which the embryonic African cinema would emerge in the post-1960s. Locals who had worked as assistants under European directors moved to positions behind cameras. Funding and training opportunities offered by former colonial powers, namely France through its Ministry of Cooperation's film development programs, played a critical role in the preeminence of cinema in independent francophone West African countries from the 1960s to the 1980s relative to other parts of sub-Saharan Africa, with the exception of South Africa. In contrast to France, the UK has not heavily invested in the development of cinema production in its former colonies after they gained political independence. The British colonial rule of association meant less involvement than was the case of French assimilation policies or direct rule. As for Lusophone Africa, the strong tradition of the documentary genre reflects the historical use of film as an instrument in the liberation wars against Portugal.

The conception and use of the filmic medium as a propagandist tool led to the development of educational and ethnographic films from the mid-1930s to the early 1960s by the colonial powers of France, the UK, and Belgium. These short educational films targeted indigenous audiences in order to teach them about better agricultural techniques and basic hygienic practices. Such films produced by the French in Upper Volta include *Paysans noirs ou Famoro le tyran* (1947) by Georges Regnier and *Opération arachides* (1962) and *Culture attelée et fertilisation* (1964) by Serge Ricci. As indicated earlier, these kinds of productions cut across different colonized territories. The online "Colonial Film: Moving Images of the British Empire" database showcases many examples of these didactic movies, such as *Fight Tuberculosis in the Home* (1946), shot in Ghana and Nigeria, *Mengo Hospital* (1930), which features vaccination in Uganda, and *Tropical Hookworm* (1930) in Tanganyika.

A second category of educational and ethnographic films was designed for the *métropole* audience to serve as justification for continued support for the colonial project. The timing of these genres of movies is revealing of the sociopolitical changes occurring in Europe such as in France.

> Apparently, French audiences were in dire need of edification on the work of imperialism in the overseas territories, perhaps suggesting that after the horrors of the Second World War, public opinion was less in favor of France's remaining a colonial power.
>
> (Genova, 2013, 33)

The common thread running through films targeted at both indigenous and metropolitan audiences is the ideological underpinning premised on the idea of superiority, which serves as a reason to subjugate others to its own model. The deployment of this sense of superiority through a number of acts of oppression arguably lays bare the contradictions of this ideology.[3] It is also important to underline the fact that priests were actively involved in the making and exhibition of didactic films.

In addition to educational films, there is a corpus of productions made against the backdrop of Africa as 'exotic scenery.' In this category of films, we find ethnographic films focusing on 'otherness' and commercial Hollywood productions set in beautiful landscapes with abundant fauna. These movies certainly target the Western audiences who are receptive to narratives of exoticism and escape because the historical context of subjugation at the time was not conducive to enabling Africans' access to cinema as an entertainment medium. Ethnographic movies featuring 'otherness' include productions such as Jean Rouch's 1955 *Les maîtres fous*, on possession rites among the Hauka in Accra (Ghana), and *African Home Life* (1945), produced by East Africa Command—Directorate of Education, which focuses on Kenyan tribal dances of the Luo, Nandi, and Turkana. These two productions were made from the perspective of the outsider looking into a different culture, so they do not go beyond the exotic aspect to present complex characters. In addition to these ethnographic films that are very often produced or commissioned by the colonial powers or simply the work of private individuals documenting their experiences in Africa, certain big-budget Hollywood productions contributed to the representation of the 'dark' continent as a land of exotic adventure: *The African Lion* (James Algar, 1955), *African Treasure* (Ford Beebe, 1952), and *The African Queen* (John Huston, 1951). In these Hollywood movies, we note the recurrence of three figures whose encounter drives the narrative structure: the hunter, the blonde, and the native Africans. The interplay of these figures to showcase alterity is evident in productions such as *King Solomon's Mines* (Bennett and Marton, 1950), *Sanders of the River* (Korda, 1935), and the *Tarzan* franchise[4] movies. This type of alterity-centered entertainment movies built around adventure narratives continues to appeal to audiences, considering the numerous remakes and reboots of the *Indiana Jones* franchise movies.

The audience and distribution companies of film in colonial times provide not only great insights into understanding the economic and political contexts of the early years of cinema in Africa, but also how to read the present-day situation of African cinema in relation to the history of the medium. In terms of accessibility and scale of importance, the audience could be divided into three distinct groups: the white settler communities, the growing population of educated black people living in the cities, and the rural areas reached through different cine-mobile initiatives that provided open-air screenings and led discussions with the audience. The uneven access to movies among these categories of audience brings to the fore the economics of the nascent film industry as well as the didactic dimension of film, which would later be closely connected to African cinema. The educational screenings seemed to target audiences in remote areas of the colonies where the majority of the population lived, thus reinforcing the didactic function of filmmaking. However, it is important to be cognizant that people in rural areas did not unquestioningly absorb the content, as the

Malian intellectual and historian Amadou Hampâté Bâ recounts in his
first-person narrative "Le dit du cinéma africain" ("A Tale of African
Cinema"). Hampâté Bâ is a novelist, diplomat, and a scholar who is
known for his extensive work on the culture and history of the Fulani
people. "A Tale of African Cinema" details his village's first encounter with cinema. He starts his story with the following: "I no longer
remember exactly the first film that I saw, but I remember perfectly
well the first film screening that took place in my village. In 1908, a
European came to Bandiagara [Mali] to show a film."[5] Hampâté Bâ
goes on to underline how ignorance pushed the village elders to deny
women and children access to the screening, while most of the elders
who did attend closed their eyes during the entire movie. For the villagers, cinema was perceived as devilish, with potentially corruptive
powers at the morality level. In addition to its anthropological value,
the story shows the population's initial resistance to the cinema, which
is seen as an apparatus from outside. Eventually, this initial resistance
subsided under the pressure of the colonial administration, and most
importantly, the creation of distribution channels that contributed to
making cinema more 'popular.'

The establishment of distribution monopolies from Europe and
America in the embryonic African market defined the power relations
in the creative industry and continue to have a bearing on the place of
Africa in the economics of the global circulation of images today. In the
early 1920s, two Monaco companies emerged as the major film distribution entities across French-speaking Africa, and they would maintain
their monopolistic position into the 1980s. Even attempts at national-
izing the distribution circuit by countries such as Burkina Faso, Benin,
and Senegal in the 1970s were not successful in curtailing the dominant position of the Société d'Exploitation Cinématographique Africaine
(SECMA) and the Compagnie Africaine Cinématographique Industrielle
et Commerciale (COMACICO). These companies developed a system
of distribution that made them the de facto arbiters of which films were
imported and screened in cinema theaters in West African francophone
countries. Obviously, for the concerned territories that meant a lack of
sovereignty in cultural politics, but also a potential loss of financial revenue for local economic entities.

In Southern Africa, the situation was no different because "film distribution in the region was dominated by the Schlesinger Company, which
purchased films from American and British companies and circulated
them the length and breadth of South Africa, Botswana, and the two
Rhodesias" (Burns, 2015, 13). In addition to the distribution companies,
movie theaters were mostly owned and operated by Westerners, with

Figure 2.1 A flow diagram representing the historical process of cinema in Africa from the 1890s to 1960. This flow diagram was created by Boukary Sawadogo.

the exception of a few Lebanese and Indian expatriates who ran private establishments in certain countries such as Senegal. So, the entire process ranging from film import and distribution to management of movie theaters was out of Africans' control (Figure 2.1).

The history of cinema in Africa during colonial times provides context and insights into the role and place of Africa in the early years of the filmic medium. Africans' participation in filmmaking was mostly confined to playing the role of extras or porters of equipment, ironically in stories for and about Africans. It is a Western gaze about Africa without, with limited African audiences being able to identify with the images. Travelogue films depicting Europeans' adventures, short educational films commissioned by the *métropole*, and Hollywood productions set in Africa make up the most recurring genres of the time. Western domination was also evident in the distribution circuit through monopolistic control in the emerging media landscape. However, the political independence gained by most African countries in the 1960s marked a critical juncture in the appropriation of cinema by African audiovisual storytellers.

Inception of African Cinema: Appropriation of the Gaze

The political independence movements were deeply rooted in the pan-Africanist ideology meant to give voice, agency, and identity to black people on the continent and in the diaspora. Dismemberment of Africa, erasure of history, and the shared experience of oppression called for action and solidarity among black people, which led militants of Africa's political independence to take inspiration from the Harlem Renaissance movement. In this regard, leaders of the literary movement of Negritude of the 1940s, such as the politically committed poets Léopold Sédar Senghor from Senegal, Aimé Césaire from Martinique, and Léon-Gontran Damas from Guyana, laid the foundational work that influenced the pioneers of African cinema. Ousmane Sembène, regarded as the father of African cinema, started out his career as a novelist before turning to film because of the polysemic nature of the image and the potential of cinema to better engage the largely illiterate African population. So, the inception of African cinema in the 1960s should be understood within this context of militancy, which shaped Africans' appropriation of the film medium. Consciousness-raising emerged as the main function attributed to film, while the neo-realist and griot storytelling-based aesthetics provide insights into the relation between image and postcolonial reality.

In addressing the historical development of sub-Saharan African cinema from the 1960s to the 1990s, a particular emphasis is made on the pioneers, the characteristic traits of the film corpus of the period, and the institutional framework through the creation of the Pan-African Film and Television Festival of Ouagadougou (FESPACO).

What I refer to as pioneers of African cinema are these directors whose films in the 1960s laid the foundation of the embryonic moving image arts on the continent. The Senegalese director Ousmane Sembène is a major figure who profoundly shaped the aesthetics and themes of African cinema for half a century through consistent output of high-quality films ranging from his short *Borom Sarret* (1963), to his first feature *Black Girl* (1966), to *Moolaadé* (2004). *Black Girl* was the first sub-Saharan African film to gain international recognition. Sembène, the 'elder' as he is fondly referred to among his fellow African directors, represents the figure of the politically committed artist who fights for the political and cultural liberation of his people. In terms of thematic treatment, Sembène's filmography falls into three categories, including reimagining the place of Africa in world history by tackling colonialism, innovative portrayal of women as resilient agents of change, and denunciation of the corrupt and ineffective postcolonial African elites. These themes are evident in films such as *Xala* (1975), *Camp de Thiaroye* (1988), *Guelwaar* (1992), *Faat Kiné* (2001), and *Moolaadé*. The sociorealist aesthetics of Sembène's works share similarities with Italian Neorealism in how everyday heroism is portrayed. The sociorealist aesthetic construction fits with the overarching framework of political and cultural liberation because the situations depicted in the films are conveyed as 'real' and are therefore likely to change minds and attitudes.

In addition to Ousmane Sembène, other pioneers include the French-Mauritanian director Med Hondo who made *Soleil Ô* (*Oh Sun*) in 1967, and Moustapha Alassane (*La mort de Gandji* in 1963, *The Return of an Adventurer* in 1966) and Oumarou Ganda (*Cabascabo*, 1969), both from Niger. Before getting behind the camera, the Nigerien directors Moustapha Alassane and Oumarou Ganda had worked as assistants or actors on films by the French director and ethnologist Jean Rouch.

Paulin Soumanou Vieyra is another Senegalese director of Beninese origin who is historically associated with the inception of African cinema. His student "short *Afrique sur Seine* (*Africa on the Seine*, 1955) is sometimes described as the foundation stone of African cinema" (Cook, 2016, 649). However, Vieyra is mostly known for his role as a film critic and historian of African cinema,[6] and most importantly his role in founding the Pan-African Federation of Filmmakers (FEPACI) in 1969. Another FEPACI founding member, South African Lionel Ngakane not only is a pioneer actor and filmmaker in his home country, but he also is considered one of the first black filmmakers in the United Kingdom, where he lived in exile until the end of apartheid. While the Africans were taking possession of the camera in the 1960s, a similar artistic and cultural movement—LA Rebellion—was taking place across the US cinematic landscape.

Coined by Clyde Taylor in 1986, the LA Rebellion refers to ethnic minority filmmakers who came out of UCLA film school with the agenda of revolutionizing the black image in film by offering an alternative to Hollywood's on-screen depictions of people of color. Zeinabu irene Davis' 2016 documentary *Spirits of Rebellion: Black Cinema from UCLA* comprehensively documents the development of this movement into the early 1990s through interviews and clips from films such as Bob Nakamura's 1971 *Manzanar, Child of Resistance* (Gerima, 1973), *Killer of Sheep* (Burnett, 1977), and *Daughters of the Dust* (Dash, 1991). The LA Rebellion drew on staging from Third Cinema and African cinema, particularly the films of Sembène Ousmane and Med Hondo (Figure 2.2).

Following the pioneers, the 1970s and 1980s saw the emergence of a generation of filmmakers that broadened cinematic expression in almost every African country. There is continuity and discontinuity in this generation's creative work as they built on and challenged their

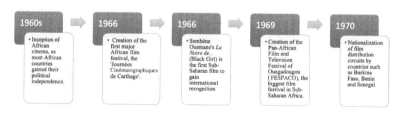

Figure 2.2 A flow diagram underlying some key historic junctures in the development of African cinemas in the 1960s and 1970s. This flow diagram was created by Boukary Sawadogo.

predecessors' filmmaking. So, political and cultural liberation narratives continued to thrive, while "return to the source" films (Diawara, 1992, 140) and an increased scrutiny of local issues were gaining more attention. These trends are evident in productions such as the Malian director Souleymane Cissé's *Baara* (1979) and *Yeelen* (1987), Ola Balogun's *Amadi* (1975) from Nigeria, *Wend Kuuni* (1982) by Gaston Kaboré from Burkina Faso, *Touki Bouki* (1973) by the Senegalese director Djibril Diop Mambéty, *Bal poussière* (1988) by the Ivorian filmmaker Henri Duparc, *Muna Moto* (1975) by Jean-Pierre Dikongue-Pipa from Cameroon, and *Yaaba* (1989) by the Burkinabe director Idrissa Ouédraogo. It should be noted that most of these cinematic productions from francophone Africa were heavily subsidized by the French Ministry of Cooperation, seeking to maintain a French sphere of influence. With the exception of a few countries such as Burkina Faso, Senegal, and Benin that had attempted to nationalize film distribution circuits, African audiences had limited opportunities to see their own images. In this regard, Olivier Barlet described the situation of African cinema as an audience without a market that has developed "in the North's shadow" (2010, 81). It was also during the 1970s and 1980s that the first African women filmmakers made an entry into the male-dominated environment of audiovisual storytelling. Safi Faye from Senegal made *Lettre Paysanne* (*A Farmer's Letter*) in 1975 and *Sambizanga* was released in 1972 by the French director of African descent Sarah Maldoror, who is regarded as one of the prominent African female filmmakers.

From the 1990s to the 2020s: The Rise of Nollywood, Intervention of Transnational Media Giants, Streaming, and Local TV Serials

The 1990s represent a key juncture in the development of African cinemas, which were shaped by technological innovation (video) and the end of one-party rule in many countries. The combined effect of these changes led to a greater democratization of the film medium, as many storytellers could use inexpensive video technologies to make movies instead of the industry standard of 35 mm, which was costly in terms of film stock purchase and editing costs. A video-camera, a computer, and editing software became the basic equipment needed by a filmmaker to produce what is referred to as 'home videos' or 'video movies' in countries such as Nigeria, Ghana, Kenya, Uganda, and Tanzania. These are shoestring budget movies that necessitate less time and personnel commitment. The documentary *Welcome to Nollywood* (Meltzer, 2007) takes the viewer into Nigeria's film industry, which churns out hundreds of films weekly. Academics and film critics may lament the poor acting or pictorial qualities, but the general public is always eager to connect with their own stories on screen. Nollywood is Nigeria's mostly video-driven productions in English and Yoruba languages that are distributed locally, but also internationally through well-crafted strategies that Noah Tsika explores in his 2015 book *Nollywood Stars: Media and Migration in West Africa and the Diaspora.* The advent of video technologies has revolutionized filmmaking and the distribution of content in Africa. Accessibility and proximity best describe the relation between the storyteller and the medium, as well as the local viewer's relation to the image.

The streaming market in Africa features several transnational media companies, including Showmax, Netflix, Apple, Amazon Prime Video, Disney+, and MUBI. The intervention of Netflix, Amazon Prime Video, Disney+, and Apple Studios has so far taken the form of exclusive licensing deals of movies that already had cinema runs, multiproject development, and production of African originals in collaboration with African directors and studios. Film and television projects range from historical drama to action series to animated series. Serialization of content is one of the characteristic traits of these streaming giants for their subscription-based economic model, which is certain to have an impact on aesthetics, form, and format across productions.

The fastest growing sectors in the African screen media landscape today include TV serials, animated films and series, and gaming. Locally produced African TV series or shows and Netflix African originals (*Queen Sono, Blood & Water*, and *Savage Beauty*) are expanding the reach of African screen media productions to wider audiences. The shift to digital terrestrial television from analog television broadcasting and the corporate intervention of streaming giants in Africa have significantly changed the landscape of distribution and exhibition of films and TV serials on the continent since the 2010s. From their initial roles as distributors, several of the transnational media companies have also increasingly become producers and funders of content, strengthening their grip on different parts of the production and distribution chain of African audiovisual content. That is the case of Netflix, Disney+, Amazon, Canal+, and TV5Monde. The French Canal+, through its Abidjan-based subsidiary A+, which was created in 2014, is co-producer, funder, and distributor of a large segment of French-speaking African serials, which are made in such a formatted content that they often lack diversity and nuances beyond national or local settings. In addition, TV5Monde, the French-language cable television that broadcasts on several continents, is also a major funder and distributor of African serials (Figure 2.3).

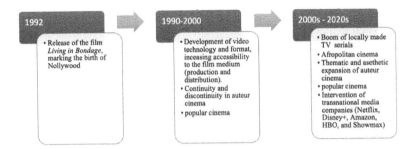

Figure 2.3 A flow diagram representing some key markers in African screen media productions between the 1990s and 2020s. From the rise of Nollywood to the intervention of transnational media and entertainment companies (Netflix, Disney+, Amazon, HBO, Apple, and Showmax), and TV serials in African screen media sectors. This diagram was created by Boukary Sawadogo.

Case Study: Sanders of the River *(Zoltan Korda, 1935): Celebration of the British Empire*

Sanders of the River (1935) is the first Africa-themed movie by the critically acclaimed Hungarian-born filmmaker Zoltan Korda, who has worked in Hollywood and in the UK with his brother Alexander's London Films production company. Most of Zoltan Korda's films are set in Africa or India. In addition to *Sanders of the River*, his other films set in Africa include *Sahara* (1943), *Cry, the Beloved Country* (1951), and *Storm over the Nile* (1955). Set in the 1930s in the British colony of Nigeria, *Sanders of the River* celebrates the British Empire through the protagonist Sanders (locally know as Sandi), the district commissioner, who represents law and order among warring tribes in West Africa. The nature of the film as a tribute to colonialism is conveyed through the 'othering' narrative and the 'infantilization' of Africans to justify the need to pacify them.

The Othering Narrative

Films depicting Africa as an exotic place usually follow the same narrative patterns of a safari trip, treasure hunt, or adventurer's journey leading to the discovery or experience of cultural differences coupled with breath-taking landscapes and fauna. However, for *Sanders of the River*, the escapist approach is not the primary focus as it seeks to justify the colonial project to the intended Western audience in simplistic binary oppositions. This film is constructed on the idea of the frontier, with the oppositions of civilization versus primitiveness, order versus lawlessness, and whites versus natives. In this respect, the film shares similarities with classical Hollywood or spaghetti westerns in the portrayal of settlers versus native Americans and the underlying civilizing mission. The African subjects are depicted as primitives in their practices and garments, and technically inferior to the colonial administrators who have firearms and navigate the river on a steamboat. For instance, Sanders warns Bosambo, played by Paul Robeson, against the promiscuity of polygamous practice by extolling the Christian values of monogamy. In the film, the outsiders have the power of labeling and determining what would be in the best interests of the indigenous population. Bosambo, a convict who ran away from Liberia, has usurped the title of king of the Ochori tribe, and will later be imposed by Sanders as ruler of the territory of King Mofolaba. This power of decision and categorization further underlines the othering authority that lies with the outsiders. Concerning languages spoken in the film, the differentiated treatment creates a hierarchy between African and English languages. For instance, whenever a local language is spoken, the message "speaking of a foreign language" invariably appears on the screen, though diegetic characters like the officers appear to perfectly understand the local languages. No efforts are made to partially translate local languages, either in the diegetic world through the local translators working for colonial officers, or in postproduction. Similarly, in the film *King Solomon's Mines* (Compton Bennett and Andrew Marton, 1950), the "speaking tribal language" systematically comes on screen when a native language is spoken. The messages and nuances in communication are lost through the homogenizing "speaking of a foreign language" and "speaking tribal language," which establishes a hierarchy among languages but most significantly points to who is the target audience.

The Infantilization of African Subjects

The infantilization of African subjects by the colonizers is designed to justify and rationalize the reasons for domination to themselves and to the locals. Portraying Africans as incapable of holding responsibilities and needing supervision only justifies the need for intervention. This is evident in a scene where the departing Sanders summons all the kings and chiefs for their pledge of allegiance to the interim district commissioner Fergusson because he is leaving for London on a one-year leave to get married. The shot composition and the message delivered to the African traditional leaders leave no shred of doubt as to who is in charge. A panning long shot shows Sanders pacing back and forth in front of the kings and chiefs who are lined up on the right of the frame, and then he says: "I want you to obey him [Fergusson] as if you were all his children" (37:30).

All agreed to keep the peace and behave responsibly in the absence of
Sanders. However, shortly after Sanders' departure, King Mofolaba's
warriors abduct King Bosambo's wife, which is regarded as an act of war
by all parties. The rumored death of Sanders relayed by sounds of drums,
which is initiated by Mofolaba's warriors, threatened to further create
chaos in the region as Fergusson is not feared and respected by locals
like Sanders. Informed of the impending all-out war, Sanders returns
to the region to quell the rivalries and restore peace. The news of his
return is relayed over drums: "Sandi is not dead. The law is back on the
river" (56:25). So, Sanders, the district commissioner, is portrayed as the
father figure that provides stability and wisdom to quarreling kingdoms
and chiefdoms, particularly in the context of King Mofolaba's ambition
to rule the other territories. The film portrays Africa as if there were no
established local practices of negotiation or peaceful mechanisms to set-
tling disagreements before the arrival of the colonizer. The representation of tribes in perpetual conflict also shows a disregard for or lack of
knowledge of precolonial West African history regarding trade relations
(trans-Saharan trade routes), and knowledge and science dissemination
centers (Timbuktu, Kano, Borno) across chiefdoms and kingdoms.

The Celebration of the British Empire

The juxtaposition of the opening two shots contextualizes the making
and intended purpose of the film, which is to commend the unsung
work by British Empire servants like Sanders. The film opens on a shot
of the British flag floating in the background, with white lettering on the
screen that reads:

> Sailors, soldiers and merchant-adventurers were the pioneers who
> laid the foundation of the British Empire. Today this is carried on by
> the Civil Servants—keepers of the King's Peace.
>
> (2:45)

Then, the screen fades out to the next message:

> Africa …
> Tens of millions of natives under British rule, each tribe with its own
>   chieftain, governed and protected by a handful of white men whose
>   everyday work is an unsung saga of courage and efficiency.
> One of them was Commissioner Sanders.
>
> (3:07)

Through its opening shots, the othering discourse, and the infantilization representational device, the film celebrates the British Empire as an enterprise that provides law, order, and civilization to people of the river who are undermined by rivalries among local kings and slave raids. Obviously, the British intervention gives limited creditability to local political structures or practices unless they serve the interests of the empire.

Notes

1 Individual and collective representations of reality based on shared beliefs, images, visions, cosmology, and so on.
2 "[T]he absence of our [African] image in the mirror," an observation made by Balufu Bakupa-Kanyinda in his closing remarks at the CODESRIA's workshop at the 2017 FESPACO in Ouagadougou on February 28, 2017.
3 For instance, the West claims the superiority of its civilization and uses it as a reason to oppress other people, which in turn negates that claimed moral superiority because civilized people would not subjugate others.
4 The first Tarzan movie, *Tarzan of the Apes*, was directed by Scott Sidney in 1918.
5 Translation by Beti Ellerson at www.africanwomenincinema.org/AFWC/A_tale _of_African_cinema.html.
6 Vieyra's notable books are *Le cinéma et l'Afrique* (1969) and *Le cinéma africain: des origines à 1973*, which was published in 1975.

Bibliography and Filmography

Ashbury, Roy, Wendy Helsby, and Maureen O'Brien. *Teaching African Cinema.* London: British Film Institute, 1998.

Bâ, Amadou Hampâté. "Le dit du cinema africain." In *Premier catalogue sélectif international de films ethnographiques sur l'Afrique noire*, ed. UNESCO, 9–19. Bruges: Les Presses Saint-Augustin, 1967.

Bachy, Victor. *La Haute-Volta et le cinéma.* Brussels: OCIC/Harmattan, 1983.

Barlet, Olivier. "African Filmmakers' New Strategies; From Métis to Nomadic; Cinema: An Audience without a Market; Five Decades of African Film." *Black Camera* 1, no. 2 (Summer 2010): 63–102.

Bordwell, David. *Planet Hong Kong: Popular Cinema and the Art of Entertainment.* Cambridge: Harvard University Press, 2000.

Burns, James. "The Western in Colonial Southern Africa." In *The Western in the Global South*, ed. MaryEllen Higgins, Rita Keresztesi, and Dayna Oscherwitz, 11–23. New York and London: Routledge, 2015.

Burns, James. *Cinema and Society in the British Empire, 1895–1940.* New York: Palgrave Macmillan, 2013.

Centre d'Enseignement et de Recherche Audio Visuels. *Le cinéma en Côte d'Ivoire.* Abidjan, Côte d'Ivoire: Université Nationale de Côte d'Ivoire, 1986.

Cook, David A. *A History of Narrative Film*. 5th ed. New York: W. W. Norton, 2016.

Diawara, Manthia. *African Cinema: Politics and Culture*. Bloomington: Indiana University Press, 1992.

Genova, James E. *Cinema and Development in West Africa*. Bloomington and Indianapolis: Indiana University Press, 2013.

Mazierska, Ewa. "Introduction: Marking Political Cinema." *Framework: The Journal of Cinema and Media* 55, no. 1 (Spring 2014): 33–44.

Sanders of the River. Dir. Zoltan Korda. The Criterion Collection, 1935.

Solanas, Fernando, and Octavio Getino. "Toward a Third Cinema." *Cinéaste* 4, no. 3 (1970–1971): 1–10. http://www.colonialfilm.org.uk/.

Tsika, Noah. *Nollywood Stars: Media and Migration in West Africa*. Bloomington: Indiana University Press, 2015.

Vieyra, Soumanou Paulin. *Le cinéma africain des origines à 1973*. Paris: Présence Africaine, 1975.

Vieyra, Soumanou Paulin. *Le cinéma et l'Afrique*. Paris: Présence Africaine, 1969.

Suggested Readings and Films

Amandla. Dir. Nerina De Jager. Netflix, 2022.

Bakari, Imruh. "African Film in the 21st Century: Some Notes to a Provocation." *Communication Cultures in Africa* 1, no. 1 (2018): 8–27.

Bisschoff, Lizelle. *Africa's Lost Classics: New Histories of African Cinema*. New York: Routledge, 2014.

Botha, Martin. *South African Cinema, 1896–2010*. Bristol and Chicago: Intellect, 2012.

Ebrahim, Haseenah, and Jordache A. Ellapen. "Cinema in Postapartheid South Africa: New Perspectives." *Black Camera* 9, no. 2 (2018): 169–176.

Harrow, W. Kenneth, and Carmela Garritano. *A Companion to African Cinema*. Hoboken: Wiley Blackwell, 2018.

Maingard, Jacqueline. *South African National Cinema*. London and New York: Routledge, 2008.

Nothing but the Truth. Dir. John Kani. 2009.

Tsika, Noah. *Cinematic Independence: Constructing the Big Screen in Nigeria*. Oakland: University of California Press, 2022.

Sawadogo, Boukary. *West African Screen Media: Comedy, TV Series, and Transnationalization*. East Lansing: Michigan State University Press, 2019.

3 Parallel Movement

African Cinemas and African American Cinema

When black British actors of Nigerian and Ugandan descent played African American characters in a number of movies, it was met with criticism from African Americans in the film industry such as the actor and producer Samuel L. Jackson and the actress Cicely Tyson. The film *Harriet* (Kasi Lemmons, 2019) features Cynthia Erivo playing Harriet Tubman; a young African American male in Jordan Peele's *Get Out* (2017) is played by Daniel Kaluuya; and David Oyelowo was cast as Martin Luther King Jr. in *Selma* (Ava DuVernay, 2014). The reaction to these black British actors points to several larger issues, including competition for opportunities, who gets to claim blackness in America, and who gets to tell whose story. However, this situation can also be considered in another larger context, specifically the relations between Africa and the diaspora. In cinema, the relations between African Americans and Africa have yet to be fully developed to their potential beyond the often-cited television and film productions of *Roots* (1977), *Coming to America* (1988), *Coming 2 America* (2021), and *Black Panther* (2018). In addition, the limited scope of the engagement of Africans and African Americans is evidenced by several examples: Danny Glover playing in and also producing African(-related) movies such as *Bamako* (Abderrahmane Sissako, 2006) and *Concerning Violence* (Göran Olsson, 2014); Forest Whitaker in *Last King of Scotland* (Kevin Macdonald, 2006); rapper Saul Williams playing Satché in *Tey* (Today, 2012) by Franco-Senegalese director Alain Gomis; and the recent forays of Will Smith's Westbrook Studios into African cinemas to produce film and television projects. However, it is hard to name the few African-born actors who are cast in films made by African Americans. The Ivorian actor Isaac De Bankolé and films by Ethiopian director Haile Gerima provide some threads of conversation between Africa and African Americans in cinema (Figure 3.1).

When the Marvel movie *Black Panther*, directed by Ryan Coogler, was released in theaters in mid-February 2018, the reception was tremendous

DOI: 10.4324/9781003246763-4

Figure 3.1 Boukary Sawadogo at the opening week of *Black Panther* at the AMC
Empire Theater, Times Square, New York City.

across generations of cinephiles in the United States. Social media posts
showed moviegoers donned in African dress on the Thursday and Friday
opening nights of *Black Panther*. The movie, for the duration of its runtime
or shortly after, has brought excitement and pride upon its African roots.
No recent production has had such a public resonance since the 1977
miniseries *Roots*, which chronicles the story of the teenager Kunta Kinte,
who was brought to America from Africa for enslavement. The black
stars in the cast from different backgrounds acting in a superhero film
has certainly contributed to the good audience reception. *Black Panther*
exemplifies the power and polysemic nature of the image, particularly
in collapsing space and time around the sharing of black experience. As
screen media consumers, how often do we generally come across cultural
productions such as *Black Panther* that connect and touch black diasporic
communities beyond geographical borders? For that matter, where do we
see convergence and divergence in African and African American cultural
productions, particularly their cinematic works? What is black cinema?

Before delving into the analysis of African and African American cinema, it is important to first address the challenges of defining what it means to be black in relationship to creative productions. Separated physically by the transatlantic divide over 400 years, Africa and the black diaspora have often developed cultural productions that reflect concerns and realities particular to each group. In the process, different historical and cultural referents are developed to better situate each group within its environment. In this situation, what could possibly bring together these two worlds, especially their cultural productions, into a comparative framework? One could perhaps venture with an answer that given their historiographies, a discourse on trauma and resistance to oppressive power structures may be the most suitable reading lens. Except that such an approach could lead to the slippery and controversial terrain of attempting to establish equivalencies in suffering, which is not welcome nor the argument in this chapter. What about African heritage then? It could well serve as the entry point into a conversation between African and African American cultural productions, but one should also be mindful that African heritage is not experienced and assumed the same way by everyone. In this respect, another layer of conceptual challenges concerns the reconfiguration of diasporic identity and imaginaries, as exemplified in W.E.B. Du Bois' notion of African American "double consciousness" of being American and Negro (*The Souls of Black Folk*, 1903), and the rhizome identity developed by Edouard Glissant to explain how identity in the black Caribbean has many roots, with Africa being just one of them. So, identity is shaped and developed in relationship to places. In addition, other intellectuals such as Frantz Fanon have also theorized on the fragmented identity and psychological trauma of oppressed peoples. So, in consideration of the above-described differences in historic and cultural referents, and identity construction, we might wrongly assume that, for instance, *Black Panther* is an exception that confirms the premise of no direct engagement between Africans and African Americans in the production of audiovisual productions.

In reality, there is a longstanding tradition in the intellectual and cultural exchange between Africa and the African American diaspora. Marcus Garvey's black nationalist Universal Negro Improvement Association (UNIA) proclaimed a "Black to Africa" message in the 1920s, while the Harlem Renaissance movement influenced the birth and development of the Negritude literary movement (Léopold Sédar Senghor, Aimé Césaire, and Léon Gontran Damas). Negritude helped lay the intellectual and theoretical groundwork for the anticolonial and liberation discourse in the struggle for political independence in Africa. The 1960s witnessed a *rapprochement* of certain civil rights movement leaders with Africa, Malcolm X's trips to Africa to meet with Gamal Abdel Nasser and Kwame Nkrumah, while some Black Panther leaders lived in exile in Algeria and Tanzania. Today, the transatlantic flows of ideas are still present through the works of writers such as Chimamanda Ngozi Adichie and Nnedi Okorafor, and university professors like Manthia Diawara, Mamadou Diouf, Achille Mbembe, and Souleymane Bachir Diagne. Beyond the intellectual circles, it is important to point out that influences of African culture are present throughout the diaspora in areas of spirituality, cuisine, architecture, music, fashion, and cinema.

Black Cinema: Points of Contact between African Cinemas and African American Film

The historical developmental timelines of African and African American cinema run parallel to each other, but also share similarities in their status as (oppositional) cinema outside the mainstream, the search for creative voices in the 1960s, and co-productions involving actors across the Atlantic. The birth of African American cinema can be traced back to the late 1910s with the emergence of race films, while the inception of African cinema is closely connected with African countries gaining their political independence in the 1960s. There is a historical period gap of almost 50 years between them, but it should be noted that African experiences of early cinema date back to the late 19th and early 20th centuries when the first films and studios were built on the continent (Harrow, 2017, x–xi). The appropriation of the film medium to craft one's own stories served as impetus to the creation of these two cinemas. The creation of African cinema in the context of political and cultural liberation enabled the continent to contradict the stereotypical and demeaning depictions of Africans from colonial cinema, just as race films' reaction to the portrayal of African Americans in D.W. Griffith's *The Birth of a Nation* (1915). In the latter, the infantilization of black characters is coupled with their depiction as morally dubious and criminals (with an obsession with the white woman). In reaction to these reductive representations, black directors such as Oscar Micheaux, Spencer Williams, Richard E. Norman, Noble and George Johnson, and Richard C. Kahn produced films that uplifted black people—race films. These films were made for black audiences by black directors with predominantly black casts: *Within Our Gates* (1920) and *Body and Soul* (1925) both by Oscar Micheaux, *The Flying Ace* (Richard E. Norman, 1926), *The Scar of Shame* (Frank Perugini, 1927), and *The Blood of Jesus* (Spencer Williams, 1941).

As African cinema came into existence in the early 1960s, replacing colonial cinema with its own production structures and discourse, the

African American cinema output decreased during the same period, in relative contrast to its sustained period of production from the 1920s through the 1950s. This decrease in output could be attributed to the start of the civil rights movements and also to the fact that perhaps race films had begun by then to lose black audiences to Hollywood. Interestingly, the 1960s are a key historical juncture that brought the two expressions of black cinema closer, as the embryonic African cinema and the LA Rebellion were each seeking creative ways to better render blackness (black experience and aesthetics) in film. Ousmane Sembène's 1966 *La Noire de …* (Black Girl) and Med Hondo's *Soleil Ô* (Oh Sun! 1967) address both the topical issue of Africans' migration to France, with the underlying narrative of alienation being an important component that could resonate with African Americans' experience of segregation. Aesthetically, Sembène made insightful creative choices in his film to depict the alienation of the protagonist Diouana through voice-over narration, music, and space as markers of marginalization. Similarly, the search for a new form is evident in *Soleil Ô* (Oh Sun!) in how the film features elements of Russian formalism in the editing by linking different themes. The thematic treatment of alienation and racism endured by black people, and the exploration of new creative forms, were particularly appealing to the group of minority students enrolled in UCLA film school. Sharing the same sensibility, the work of those audiovisual storytellers is collectively referred to as the 'LA Rebellion,' a term coined by the film scholar Clyde Taylor. The minority students were initially recruited into the UCLA Ethno-Communication program as part of efforts to engage with communities of color in the aftermath of the Watts riots in 1965. The Ethiopian film scholar Teshome H. Gabriel has been a teacher and mentor to many of these students at UCLA. The LA Rebellion is an oppositional cinema by a group of black filmmakers and media artists who sought to present different images and stories of black people beyond the often generalizing depictions of minorities in Hollywood cinema. In the documentary *Spirits of Rebellion: Black Cinema from UCLA* (Zeinabu irene Davis, 2016), which provides an intimate insight into the movement from within, members referred to the work of Ousmane Sembène and Med Hondo as a source of inspiration in their formative years.

The study of the cartographies in the cross-pollination of African and American cinema can also help to unearth the multiple lines of connection between the two cinemas. Productions featuring African or African American actors in stories set in the United States or on the continent provide the tools to map out these cartographies of intersectionality. *Sanders of the River* (Zoltan Korda, 1935) provides some of the earliest historical evidence of an African American cast portraying Africans in Africa-themed movies, with Paul Robeson and Mae McKinney as natives of the British colony of Nigeria. Other more recent productions include Morgan Freeman playing Nelson Mandela in the 2009 *Invictus* by Clint Eastwood, Forest Whitaker being cast as Idi Amin in *The Last King of Scotland* (Kevin Macdonald, 2007), Danny Glover in Abderrahmane Sissako's 2006 *Bamako*, and Don Cheadle in *Hotel Rwanda* (Terry George, 2004). On the other side of the Atlantic are the Africa-themed movies that are set in the United States such as *Coming to America* (John Landis, 1988) in which Eddie Murphy plays an African prince in New York City, and African-directed films on the experience of African immigrant communities such as *Little Senegal* (Rachid Bouchareb, 2001), *Restless City* (Andrew Dosunmu, 2011), and *Mother of George* (Andrew Dosunmu, 2013). The notable observations that transpire from the two cinematic practices concern how African-directed films set in the United States tend to come from independent/auteur cinema, while African-themed films featuring African American casts are very often from Hollywood productions. Interestingly, parallels could be established between African American cinema and African cinema in how they both operate as forms of independent cinema in producing and distributing outside mainstream channels. However, they sometimes seem to be moving past one another, with no sizable and well-crafted zones of contact—hence the parallel movement. More lines of communication certainly need to be opened in the film industry, enabling stakeholders of African and African American cinema to exchange creative ideas and to create joint ventures in production and distribution. In general, only a relatively limited number of sub-Saharan African actors such as Djimon Hounsou, Issach de Bankolé, Omar Sy, and Lupita Nyong'o have had some success in Hollywood. The current cartographies show instead the picture of individual productions with limited connections that can be drawn among them regarding themes, aesthetics, and types of productions. In terms of content or narrative about these individual productions, the relationship between Africa and the black diaspora is often not addressed substantially, with the few exceptions of *Roots*, *Little Senegal*, and *Black Panther*. Although, examples of co-productions between Africans and African Americans are currently limited relative to their potential, Danny Glover and Forest Whitaker have been particularly active over the past years in producing films on/about Africa. For instance, Danny Glover has coproduced the documentary *Concerning Violence* (Göran Hugo Olsson, 2014) on the liberation struggles in Africa in the 1960s and 1970s. Glover is particularly drawn to productions that have a high potential of public educational value to black people, which is the case of *The Black Power Mixtape 1967–1975*

(Göran Hugo Olsson, 2011), which he coproduced. He has also been working on the production of a film on the Haitian Revolution leader Toussaint Louverture. As for African coproduction initiatives, there is, for instance, "The Filmmakers Association of Nigeria, USA, a project intended to organize the American market and encourage crossover projects" (Haynes, 2016, 237).

In addition, the festival distribution circuit represents another zone of contact where African and African American films coexist in the same space, which could have the potential for creating a discourse around them. However, this coexistence at certain festivals has not always led to a greater engagement between the two cinemas or to scholarly productions. Besides the informal distribution networks and online platforms, African films are brought to the United States through a number of festivals featuring a lineup of international films (Tribeca Film Festival, African Diaspora International Film Festival, Anthology Film Archives, Lincoln Center, Museum of Modern Art, etc.) and cultural institutions that showcase black artistic expressions such as ImageNation, New Voices in Black Cinema, and Brooklyn Academy of Music (African festival). Since the early 1990s, and for more than a decade, California Newsreel's Library of African Cinema project has been a distribution outlet of African cinema for the academic community until it ceased acquiring any more new African titles. On the African continent, productions from the black diaspora are not well known to the general public beyond film industry and academic circles, maybe for a lack of initiatives or the systemic challenges of distribution facing African cinema. Since its 11th edition in 1989, the Pan-African Film and Television of Ouagadougou (FESPACO) has awarded the Paul Robeson Prize, named after the African American actor, singer, and activist, to award the best film of the diaspora. The prize broadens the appeal of the festival, but most significantly attempts to bridge the transatlantic divide.

Teaching Africanfuturism and Afrofuturism and African American Cinema in the Classroom

While there should be more college-level courses on African cinema, there are far fewer course offerings on African cinemas and African American cinema which bring them into conversation or dialogue. Africanfuturism and Afrofuturism may be considered as a course offering on African cinemas and African American cinema. Africanfuturism and Western-centered Afrofuturism offer frameworks showcasing the intersectionality of struggles, suffering, possibilities, and locating one's place in the world from different black experiences. The imagination of alternate realities from black and African perspectives is not only significantly important for communities of color who have endured erasure and denigration of their past, but also narratively interesting for the case of African films which are predominantly set in the past or the present. Centuries of physical separation caused by slavery and the ensuing development of each community's historic and cultural references have found ways to coexist, and even sometimes blend in future-set films. Speculative fiction can be and often is the vehicle of collapsing time and space in both African diaspora cinema and African cinemas to render differentiated black experiences in their proximity and encounters.

For your consideration, here are suggestions for a thematic organization of your course syllabus:

• Displacement of Black Roots and Culture

Last Angels of History (John Akomfrah, 1996)

• Aesthetic Constructions: Fiction or Reality?

Naked Reality (Jean-Pierre Bekolo, 2016)

• Female Change Agents in Postcolonial Africa

Les Saignantes (Bloodettes, 2007) by Jean-Pierre Bekolo

• Migration in Reverse

Africa Paris (Sylvestre Amoussou, 2006)

• African Cities

Air Conditioner (2020) by Mario Bastos (known as Fradique) or District 9 (Neill Blomkamp, 2009)

• Environmental Degradation

Pumzi (Wanuri Kahiu, 2009)

• Africa Leading

Black Panther (Ryan Coogler, 2018)

Case Study: **Black Is King *(Beyoncé, 2020)***

The rationale for the selection of Beyoncé's visual album *Black Is King* as a case study is based on the intersection of music, popular culture, and cinema in showing the black experience, bringing into conversation the black diaspora and Africa. Also, *Black Is King*, adapted from *The Lion King* (1994 and 2019), is the kind of visual performance and storytelling that is different from classical performance in movies. In so many ways, *Black Is King* presents narrative parallels with *The Lion King*.

The production features stunning visuals with symbolic and literal meanings, and star-studded participation from performers and artists such as Beyoncé, Jay-Z, Lupita Nyong'o, Pharrell Williams, Yemi Alade, Kelly Rowland, Naomi Campbell, Nyaniso Dzedze, Blitz (Bazawule) the Ambassador, Wizkid, Warren Masemola, Mary Twala, and Stephen Ojo.

The plot of *Black Is King* is built around a young prince Simba who is exiled from his African homeland, followed with questions of identity and heritage as he seeks ways to take back his crown, which finally happens with the guidance of his ancestors. The narrative mirrors the history of the transatlantic slave trade in which millions of enslaved Africans were forcefully removed from their homes. Then, slaves and their descendants suffered systematic exploitation and dehumanization for centuries. *Black Is King* is an ode to blackness, celebrating African heritage and bringing into conversation Africa and the diasporas around culture. Upon its release, viral twitter discussions were split over cultural appropriation for capitalist gains and claims that *Black Is King* fossilizes Africa in times of past kingdoms with no regard to contemporary Africa. These discussions are revealing of the need to foster deep dialogue between continental Africans and the diaspora, and how audiovisual stories and artists and performers with global reach can bridge a transatlantic divide while acknowledging differences in black experience.

Black Is King offers several entry points in the examination of the nature and breadth of the relations between African cinema and African American cinema. Such examination can be articulated around the role and influence of global stars, and content form and distribution for black audiences and beyond. Another reading lens may look at how themes of black agency, migration, Afropolitanism, Afrofuturism, Africanfuturism are portrayed in (dis)similar ways. In this respect, here are some films to consider in a comparative framework:

Black Panther (Ryan Coogler, 2018)
Atlantics (Mati Diop, 2019)
Black Girl (Ousmane Sembène, 1966)

Queen of Katwe (Mira Nair, 2016)
Hidden Figures (Theodore Melfi, 2016)

Suggested Readings and Films

Bakari, Imruh. "African Film in the 21st Century: Some Notes to a Provocation." *Communication Cultures in Africa* 1, no. 1 (2018): 8–27.

Bakari, Imruh, and Mbye Cham. *African Experiences of Cinema.* London: British Film Institute, 1996.

Bogle, Donald. *Toms, Coons, Mulattoes, Mammies, & Bucks: An Interpretive History of Blacks in American Films.* 5th ed. New York and London: Bloomsbury Academic, 2016.

Burns, James. *Cinema and Society in the British Empire, 1895–1940.* New York: Palgrave Macmillan, 2013.

Concerning Violence. Dir. Göran Hugo Olsson. Kino Lorber, 2015.

Dash, Julie. *Daughters of the Dust: The Making of an African American Woman's Film.* New York: New Press, 1992.

Dery, Mark, ed. *Flame Wars: The Discourse of Cyberculture.* Durham: Duke University Press, 1994.

Diallo, Yaya, and Mitchell Hall. *The Healing Drum: African Wisdom Teachings.* Rochester: Destiny Books, 1989.

Diawara, Manthia. *Black American Cinema.* New York and London: AFI, 1993.

Field, Allyson, Jan-Christopher Horak, and Jacqueline Najuma Stewart, eds. *L.A. Rebellion: Creating a New Black Cinema.* Oakland: University of California Press, 2015.

Gillespie, B. Michael. *Film Blackness: American Cinema and the Idea of Black Film.* Durham: Duke University Press, 2016.

Guerrero, Ed. *Framing Blackness: The African American Image in Film.* Philadelphia: Temple University Press, 1993.

Haynes, Jonathan. *Nollywood: The Creation of Nigerian Film Genres.* Chicago: University of Chicago Press, 2016.

Harrow, W. Kenneth, ed. *African Filmmaking: Five Formations.* East Lansing: Michigan State University Press, 2017.

Masood, Paula. *Black City Cinema: African American Urban Experiences in Film.* Philadelphia: Temple University Press, 2003.

Okorafor, Nnedi. *Noor.* New York: DAW Books, 2021.

Pioneers of African American Cinema. Dir. Oscar Micheaux et al. Kino Lorber, 2016.

Sawadogo, Boukary. *West African Screen: Comedy, TV Series, and Transnationalization.* East Lansing: Michigan State University Press, 2019.

Wiseman, Andreas. "Will Smith & Jada Pinkett Smith's Westbrook Teams with Nigeria's EbonyLife On Film & TV Slate." https://deadline.com/2021/02/jada-pinkett-smith-will-smith-westbrook-nigeria-ebonylife-film-tv-slate-1234694457/. Published on February 16, 2021. Accessed 3/25/2022.

Part II

Aesthetics in African Cinemas

4 Cinematography
Space, Time, and Rhythm

As a stylistic element in filmmaking, cinematography could be defined as the creative camera work that the director undertakes to tell the story visually. The camera work involves decisions ranging from the type of shots (long, medium, or close-up), camera height and angles (low, eye-level, high angle), focal length of the lens (telephoto, medium, and wide-angle lenses), to static or mobile framing (the pan, tilt, tracking, or crane shot). Cinematography also encompasses shot composition—the arrangement of subjects and objects within the frame. The person charged with cinematography on a film shoot is known as the director of photography, or DP.

African cinema does not differ on the above-mentioned basic elements from other cinematic practices and traditions around the world. But African directors have developed a specific cinematography that cuts across all productions from sub-Saharan Africa and distinguishes them from the works of other countries. In this regard, it will be a generalizing claim to assert that there is a specifically African cinematography as an aesthetic trait cutting across all productions from sub-Saharan Africa. Certain cinematography trends are evident in the thematic treatment of the rural milieu and social exclusion in the works of auteur filmmakers such as Ousmane Sembène, Idrissa Ouédraogo, Pierre Yaméogo, and Gaston Kaboré.

In narratives featuring dynamics between the individual and the community, cinematography is prominently deployed as a creative device to visually construct contrasted spaces in a number of African films such as *Yaaba* (Idrissa Ouédraogo, 1989), *Yesterday* (Darrell Roodt, 2004),[1] *Delwende* (*Stand Up and Walk*; Pierre Yaméogo, 2005), and *Karmen Geï* (Joseph Ramaka Gaï, 2001). These films disproportionately use lots of long takes and long and medium shots to convey the physical and symbolic distance that separates the individual from the community. Because the focus appears to be social exclusion built around the preponderance

DOI: 10.4324/9781003246763-6

of the group, close-ups are naturally used sparingly. Consequently, long takes[2] and shots have a bearing on the rhythm of the movies, leading to generalizations about the slowness of African films in relation to relatively fast-paced Western productions.

Delwende and *Yesterday* tell the stories of women pushed to the margins of society by an invisible yet powerful center that decides when and if an individual is deemed fit to be part of the group. Obviously, the circumstances of the exclusion from the group are portrayed differently for the protagonists. In *Delwende*, Napoko is forced out of her village based on false accusations of witchcraft, whereas in *Yesterday*, the protagonist's AIDS sickness has turned her into an outcast from the community. The overwhelming number of long shots and takes in these two films also fosters, through the spatial construction of social exclusion, a deeper viewer engagement with the stories.

Long shots traditionally provide panoramic views with the subject in the foreground, providing contextual information necessary for understanding the scene or for making connections with the overall narrative at large. For instance, the long shot of the character Yesterday breathlessly and painfully walking to her medical appointment across the immense barren land under the blazing sun conveys the idea of her isolation and lack of support network. Because the subject stays on screen relatively longer in a long take, the viewer is compelled to engage more with Yesterday's long walk than s/he might otherwise have in takes of relatively short duration. Similarly, *Delwende* showcases numerous instances of long takes such as the ones depicting Napoko wandering in the bush from one village to the next, which reduce the distance between the viewer and the on-screen character, so Napoko is constantly in view and cannot be ignored.

However, it would be simplistic to assume that African films about exclusion invariably rely on a few kinds of shots to render the story cinematographically. For example, *Delwende* opens with a crane shot that shows a millet field from an eye-level angle before gradually pulling to a high angle on a group of villagers. *Karmen Geï* features several close-ups in addition to the long and medium shots, which are characteristic of social exclusion-themed films. *Karmen Geï*'s opening scene is made up of a series of close-ups of the seductive dance moves performed by the bisexual protagonist Karmen in the prison courtyard, and the intimacy scene involving Karmen and the warden, Angelique, in which the camera lingers on the nudity of two clinched female bodies. The distribution of long, medium, and close-up shots also reflects what Pfaff refers to as the opposition between communal space and individual space (1984, 50).

In addition, Pfaff and other scholars argue that African cinema lacks some elaborate camera work for a number of reasons, including the need to construct realism, to cater to a cinematographically unsophisticated audience, and because of the lack of film technicians (1984, 48). Pfaff contends that the sociorealist approach to filmmaking coupled with a largely illiterate audience account for the limited use of cinematography in Sembène's film corpus. There may be some validity to Pfaff's assessment of Sembène's mostly realist and politically committed films, but such an analysis cannot be extended to the work of the rest of the African directors. Though Sembène's legacy may be evident in African cinema, other directors have developed their own styles in diversifying their cinematic productions. In this regard, the emergence of particular African film genres such as the western,[3] (Afro)futurism,[4] and horror movies (Nollywood and Ghanaian videofilms)[5] shows the mastery of elaborate cinematography and editing.

Furthermore, the creation and development of film schools in several sub-Saharan African countries since the early 2000s ensures the availability of technicians and trained audiovisual storytellers who are attentive to stylistic elements such as cinematography, thus refuting any assumption that thematic treatment and the ideological dimension in African cinema would take precedence over other considerations in the creative process. The non-exhaustive list of these film schools includes Imagine and Institut Supérieur de l'Image et du Son, in Burkina Faso; Institut de Formation aux Techniques de l'Image et de la Communication, in Niger; the South African School of Motion Picture; the Institut Supérieur de Formation aux Métiers du Cinéma et de l'Audiovisuel, in Cameroon; and the Blue Nile Film and Television Academy, in Ethiopia.

As for rhythm, inspired by village life, it is rather slow in contrast, for instance, to Hollywood action-thriller movies in how plot events unfold quickly and the way shots are edited. The village life dictates the perceived slow space of *Yaaba*. Set in an unspecified time in a precolonial African village, the lives of the villagers are built around the alternation of rainy and dry seasons. It is a relatively busy lifestyle during the rainy season when they work hard to take care of their crops. After harvest, which marks the start of the dry season, villagers mostly stay home. Attending social events such as weddings, funerals, and baptisms are among the few instances that offer inhabitants the opportunity to go beyond the confines of their village. We see this kind of movement when Bila, his father, uncle, and Nopoko go to the market, and the scene of two villagers bringing the new bride of Bila's uncle from another village. Otherwise, adult villagers are shown either sitting in their compounds or chatting under sheds made of grass and millet branches, which are built to feed livestock during the dry season. The village appears to be functioning on its own rhythm, independent of outside influence. This can give the viewer a sense of a very slow-paced film, as the combination of static shots and long takes also shows a lack of dynamic unfolding of events because images stay longer on the screen.

Case Study: *Yaaba* (Idrissa Ouédraogo, 1989)

The award-winning *Yaaba* by the Burkinabe director Idrissa Ouédraogo tells the story of an old woman who lives outside her community because she is wrongfully accused of witchcraft. As a result, Yaaba is forced to wander on the village's periphery, and the two children, Bila and Nopoko, represent the only link between the community and the old woman. *Yaaba* demonstrates a Burkinabe cinematic tradition of the 1980s and 1990s that focuses on thematic treatments of children and social exclusion against the backdrop of timeless village life. Other films of this cinematic tradition include Gaston Kaboré's 1982 *Wend Kuuni* (*God's Gift*) and *Buud Yam* (1997), and Ouédraogo's 1990 *Tilaï* (*Law*, 1990), which is regarded as an African adaptation of the Oedipus story. Gaston Kaboré and Idrissa Ouédraogo are two of the best-known and best-regarded filmmakers from Burkina Faso.

Cinematography could be defined in technical terms regarding the various facets of camera work and how the visuals enhance the overall storytelling. It is worth noting that the two approaches to cinematography are not necessarily mutually exclusive. *Yaaba* showcases the symbiotic relationship between cinematography and thematic treatment, in other words, it is how the preponderance of certain types of shots are designed to underline a particular theme, location, or character's emotional state. Cinematography in *Yaaba* is marked by the recurrent use of long and medium shots throughout the movie, showcasing long takes and limited camera movement. Long shots, through panoramic views, reinforce the spatial exclusion of the protagonist who is shown numerous times walking between hills in a dry and austere environment. She is always by herself in the middle of nature, having to face intolerance from the rest of the village community. Yaaba's lonely life as a social outcast is often interrupted by visits from Bila and Nopoko, who are framed in long shots, depicting the wide spaces that they have to cover from their homes to visit Yaaba. The film offers limited mobile framing: the recurrent long and medium shots are made up of static shots. The lack of camera movement reflects the rigidity of the mindsets of the villagers, who are unwilling to shift their attitudes toward one of their own. Only once during the entire movie is mobile framing used in the form of a pan[6] shot, which is in the scene when Bila and Yaaba are eating grilled chicken that the former has stolen from his father. A pan from the left side of the frame to the right shows the two sitting next to a dilapidated house, with Bila teasing Yaaba, a toothless old woman enjoying chicken. This panning not only shifts spatial perspective, as various shots in mobile framings conventionally do, but most significantly provides insights into Yaaba as she opens up about how delighted she is to be referred to as "grandmother" (Yaaba) by Bila.

There are few close-ups in the film, which are devoted mostly to intimacy scenes, such as the ones involving Koudi and her husband, Noaga, or with her lover, Razougou. Intricate camera work involving height and angles is also kept to a bare minimum. For instance, the pervasive eye-level camera angle shots contrast with the only two high-angle shots of the film, showing Bila's father looking down on Yaaba and his son from a hilltop, and the opening shot of the wedding celebration.

As a whole, *Yaaba* is a perfect example of how directors choose to make economical use of the full range of cinematography in order to create readily recognizable visual patterns that are associated with themes. The simplicity and slow pace of the village lifestyle are reinforced cinematographically, and the theme of exclusion is brought to the fore in the juxtaposition of long shots featuring the protagonist and the village. In addition, *Yaaba* also demonstrates the use of cinematography that is apt to better capture and render local sociocultural realities. African filmmakers are re-appropriating their physical space in constructing their own audiovisual stories. Scholars such as André Gardies read the significance of spatial construction as an act of empowerment and independence of African storytellers against colonial-era images of the continent that were created by outsiders (1989, 36). (Re) appropriation consists of not only producing one's own images, but also inscribing the audiovisual storytelling within local spatial, temporal, and cultural markers, which could depart from dominant filmmaking practices in terms of rhythm and pace.

Rhythm, inspired by village life, is rather slow in contrast to that of Hollywood action-thriller movies, for instance, in how plot events unfold quickly and how shots are edited. Village life dictates the perceived slow pace of *Yaaba*. Set in an unspecified time in a precolonial African village, the lives of the villagers are built around the alternating rainy and dry seasons. The rainy season is relatively busy, when the villagers work hard to take care of their crops. After the harvest, which marks the start of the dry season, the villagers mostly stay home.

Notes

1 This South African movie was nominated in the Best Foreign Language Film category at the 77th Academy Awards.
2 'Long shot' is about distance, while 'long take' refers to a shot of lengthy duration (i.e., a fairly long-running take).
3 *African Western* (1992) by the Congolese director Ferdinand Batsimba, *L'or des Younga* (2006) by the Burkinabe director Boubakar Diallo, and *African Cowboy* (2013) by Rodney Charles.
4 Short film *The Day They Came* (2013) by the Nigerian Genesis Williams, *Pumzi* (2009) by Kenyan director Wanuri Kahiu, *District 9* (2009) by the South African Neill Blomkamp, *Africa Paradis* (2006) by the Beninese director Sylvestre Amoussou, *Les Saignantes* (*The Bloodettes*, 2005) by Cameroonian cineaste Jean-Pierre Bekolo, and *The Last Angel of History* (1995) by John Akomfrah from the UK/Ghana.
5 The rich corpus of witchcraft, or 'blood money,' films that is built around the intervention of occult forces in people's daily lives.
6 Movement of the camera horizontally, from right to left or vice versa.

Bibliography and Filmography

Delwende (Stand up and Walk). Dir. Pierre Yaméogo. Trigon-Film, 2005.

Gardies, André. *Cinéma d'Afrique noire Francophone: L'espace-miroir*. Paris: L'Harmattan, 1989.

Karmen Geï. Dir. Joseph Ramaka Gaï. Arte Cinema and Canal+ Horizons, 2001.

Pfaff, Françoise. *The Cinema of Ousmane Sembène: A Pioneer of African Film*. Westport: Greenwood, 1984.

Yesterday. Dir. Darrell Roodt. HBO Films, 2004.

Suggested Readings and Films

Brahimi, Denise. *Cinémas d'Afrique Francophone et du Maghreb*. Paris: Nathan, 1997.

Harrow, Kenneth W. *Space and Time in African Cinema and Cine-Scapes*. New York: Routledge, 2022.

Kane, Désiré Momar. *Marginalité et errance dans la littérature et le cinéma africains francophones*. Paris: Harmattan, 2004.

Pfaff, Françoise. *The Cinema of Ousmane Sembène: A Pioneer of African Film*. Westport: Greenwood, 1984.

Tcheuyap, Alexie. "African Cinema and Representations of (Homo)Sexuality." In *Body, Sexuality, and Gender: Versions and Subversions in African Literatures 1*, ed. Flora Veit-Wild and Dirk Naguschewski, 143–154. Amsterdam: Rodopi, 2005.

5 The African Animated Film

From the early 1960s to the present, the landscape of African animation may be divided into three generations, though there is some overlap between generations. Moustapha Alassane from Niger is to African animation what Ousmane Sembène is to live-action African cinema, the father. Alassane is in a category of his own as the first of the pioneering generation, with *Death of Gandji* (1963) considered the first postcolonial African animated film. The second generation, mostly formally trained, has been mostly active from the late 1980s to the mid-2000s, including Congolese Jean-Michel Kibushi, South African William Kentridge, Burkinabe Moustapha Dao and Cilia Sawadogo, Malian Kadiatou Konaté, and Malagasy Jiva Eric Razafindralambo. The third and current generation is made of self-taught animators who continue to perfect their art through workshops and online tutorials. The manga culture and new technological developments have shaped the emergence of this generation, which includes Abel Kouamé and Marguerite Abouet from Côte d'Ivoire, Burkinabe Serge Dimitri Pitroipa, Ugandan Raymond Malinga, and Nigerian Roye Okupe. This is also the time of the development of African gaming with Cameroonian Olivier Madiba (Kiroo Games) and Serge Abraham Thaddée from Guinea (African Heroes), among others. The current generation of African creatives is moving fluidly across genres (animation, gaming, cartoons) and transnational collaborative frameworks. The growing animation market in Africa has recently seen the intervention of Disney+ through co-production and distribution deals.

In addressing African animation, we have to be mindful of questions such as how to situate African animated film within the global animation landscape, which is dominated by studios such as Walt Disney and its subsidiary Pixar, DreamWorks, Industrial Light and Magic (ILM) Animation, and Gainax. How can African animation carve out a niche, develop its identity, and be judged by its own standards? These three questions, along with that of the relative marginality (in production, distribution, and criticism) of

DOI: 10.4324/9781003246763-7

animated film within African cinema, should be the larger framework for understanding the medium as we attempt to provide the reader with some insights. Few references are given throughout the chapter because, unlike live-action African film, there is limited scholarly investigation into African animation. So we know relatively little about its history, aesthetics, current productions, and new orientations. Archival and field research are needed to give us a comprehensive picture of the African animation medium beyond just the study of individual animators and productions, which is the object of most of the inquiries in the few existing articles.

Africa has a longstanding tradition of the production of animated films even though they have not garnered the same consistent academic and critical attention as their live-action counterparts. The production of animation on the continent dates back to 1935 in Egypt with the Frenkel brothers' animated cartoons featuring the Walt Disney-inspired character of Mish-Mish Effendi. However, the first animations in Black Africa were not produced until the early 1960s. Released during the inception period of African cinema, Nigerien director Moustapha Alassane's short animated films *La mort de Gandji* (1963) and *Bon Voyage Sim* (1966) are regarded as the first sub-Saharan African animated productions. In addition to Alassane's pioneering work and consistent productions throughout his career, the Congolese director Jean-Michel Kibushi Ndjate Wooto is arguably the second-most important figure in African cinema animation. Kibushi founded, in 1988, the Studio Malembe Maa, which has specialized in the production and distribution of animated films, as well as training young animators. Kibushi is himself a prolific director whose animated films have won prizes at festivals such as FESPACO, Festival Plein Sud, Festival of Milano, and Rencontres Internationales du Cinéma d'Animation de Wissembourg. Since the early 1990s, new voices have emerged in the field such as the Malian Mambaye Coulibaly (*Le geste de Ségou*, 1989), Canadian-Burkinabe Cilia Sawadogo (*La femme mariée à trois hommes*, 1993), Malian Kadiatou Konaté (*L'enfant Terrible*, 1993), South African William Kentridge (*Felix in Exile*, 1994), Rwandan Maurice Nkundimana (*Bana Twirinde Abadushuka*, "Children: Beware of Those Who Betray Us," 2007), Malagasy Ridha Andriantomanga (*ILM, Le savoir*, 2008), Ethiopian Ezra Wube (*Indamora*, 2009), Kenyans Just A Band (*Iwinyo Piny*, 2009), and Ng'endo Mukii (*Yellow Fever*, 2012), Ivorian Marguerite Abouet (*Aya of Yop City*, 2013), Ivorian Abel Kouamé Nguessan (*Pokou, Princesse Ashanti*, 2013), Malagasy Tojosoa Andrianarison a.k.a. Cid (*The Bee*, 2014) and Sitraka Randriamahaly (*Rough Life*, 2015), and the Nigerians Niyi Akinmolayan (*Room 315*, 2016), Adebimpe Adebambo (*Tejumade*, 2017), and Kola Olarewaju (*Dawn of Thunder*, 2017) (Figures 5.1 and 5.2).

Figure 5.1 *Black September in Kinshasa* (Jean–Michel Kibushi, 1992).

Figure 5.2 *Black September in Kinshasa* (Jean–Michel Kibushi, 1992).

Only a few animators such as Cilia Sawadogo, Ng'endo Mukii, and Jean-Michel Kibushi have received formal training. Most animators have received formal training in creative arts or film schools but, instead, most African animators are self-taught storytellers who continue to perfect their art through workshops organized by private initiatives or multilateral institutions. For instance, UNESCO launched in 2003 the Animated Africa! workshop series that trained creators of cartoons from East and South Africa to develop children's programs that truly reflect local culture and imaginations. In addition, Kibushi led the "Afrik'anim'action" training project to foster the emergence of the animation sector in the Democratic Republic of Congo and Burundi from 2009 to 2013.

As Bordwell notes in the tenth edition of *Film Art: An Introduction*, there are two categories of animation, including "animated fiction films, both short and feature-length" and "the animated documentaries, usually instructional ones" (2012, 387). Both categories are present in African cinema animation, with a particular prevalence of short fiction films and animated documentaries. Feature-length productions, such as Jean-Michel Kibushi's 2008 *Ngando, Aya of Yop City* by Marguerite Abouet and *Pokou, Princesse Ashanti* by Abel Kouamé Nguessan from Côte d'Ivoire, are rather the exceptions in the landscape of African cinema animation. The overwhelming majority of short fiction films and animated documentaries should be understood within the larger context of scarcity of funding for animation, which prompts storytellers to choose to work on short productions or educational pieces that are most likely to get institutional support.

For a widely universal film genre as animation, it is tempting to ask, "What is typically African in African cinema animation?" (Bendazzi, 2004, 24). In other words, it is about delving into interrogations about the predominant fabrication techniques, aesthetic traits, and thematic treatment within sub-Saharan African animation, which will enable a deeper understanding of this form of cultural production.

Animation is at the intersectionality of several artistic practices, including photography, drawing, sculpture, illustration, and computer technology (Callus, 2010, 58). In defining animation from the perspective of fabrication technique, it is about creating the illusion of motion for a series of drawn, paper-cut, photographed, or computer-generated images (characters and settings), or puppets. African animators use different techniques ranging from puppets, stop-motion, 2D and 3D animation, digital cutouts to drawn animation (Callus, 2010, 61). In this regard, there is no single or predominant technique that could be regarded as 'African' in African cinema animation. Technological innovation has shaped fabrication techniques, from Moustapha Alassane's animated puppets (*Kokoa*, 1985), Jean-Michel Kibushi's use of "post-production effects" in the making of his 2004 *Prince Loseno* (Callus, 2010, 56) to Kenneth Coker's 2D animations *Iwa* (2009) and *OniSe Owo* (2008). It should be noted that the traditional drawn animation and the various types of computer animations that have emerged in the 2000s are not mutually exclusive.

Thematic treatment and aesthetic constructions are characterized by a wide range of expressions, reflecting the different iterations of 'local' through African settings, stories, and perspectives. This diversity in thematic and aesthetic expressions is evident in the various articulations of African contemporary societal issues, historical references, the city as a site of sociopolitical transformations, timeless rurality, and orality as a rich source of artistic creativity. Ng'endo Mukii's *Yellow Fever* critically examines black identity through the skin bleaching phenomenon that currently affects many communities across the African continent. The city space is represented differently in Kibushi's *Kinshasa, Septembre noir* (1991) and Abouet's *Aya of Yop City*, as political violence takes center stage in the former while the latter features the cosmopolitan makeup and intermingling of a popular Abidjan neighborhood during the prosperous economic times of the 1970s in Côte d'Ivoire. The return to the source[1] (culture and identity) is not only a recurrent theme but also an aesthetic rendering of the past through the use of tales, legends, and mythologies in productions such as *Samba the Great* (Alassane, 1978), *The Toad Visits His In-Laws* (Kibushi, 1991), *Oni Se Owo* (Coker, 2008), *Iwa* (Coker, 2009), *La ruse du lièvre* (Sawadogo, 2000), *L'arbre aux enfants* (Sawadogo, 2005), and *Prince Loseno* (Kibushi, 2005). In his 2014 book, *Images & Animation: Le Cinéma d'animation en Afrique Centrale*, Guido Convents demonstrates how this trend was present in colonial cinema in Central Africa. For instance, *Les Palabres de Mbokolo*, the first animated series in the Belgian Congo, produced by Alexandre Van den Heuvel and Roger Jamar from 1952 to 1955, drew on local African tales. So the visuals, narrative structure, and settings highlight a cinematic practice that blends African storytelling and the appropriation of new technological innovation in animation.

In order to provide further entry points into African animated film, I would like to focus more on the work of Moustapha Alassane, the father of African animation, and Madagascar as a country that currently boasts one of the most prolific and consistent productions in sub-Saharan Africa since the early 2000s.

Moustapha Alassane, the Father of African Cinema Animation

The Museum of Modern Art held on May 12 to 15, 2017, in New York City, the first North American retrospective on Moustapha Alassane, (re)introducing the director to a general audience beyond academic and film critic circles. I was personally in attendance for three separate screenings, including *FVVA* (1972), *Toula, or the Water Genie* (1973), and *Moustapha Alassane, Cineaste of the Possible* (2008). The last two screenings were accompanied by the short animated fiction films *Kokoa* (2001) and *Samba the Great*. Though the programmatic emphasis in the retrospective was on the feature-length films by or about Alassane, nonetheless, his mostly short animated fiction films garnered attention. For African cinema scholars like myself, it was a pleasure to see Moustapha Alassane's work being celebrated even though he remains largely unknown to the general American public, which could also be said of African cinema in general. In the country of Disney, the father of African animation is not a household name like J. Stuart Blackton is to the birth of American animation.

Niger may be regarded as the birthplace of African animation through the pioneering work of Moustapha Alassane (1942–2015). Other countries such as the Democratic Republic of Congo, Madagascar, Côte d'Ivoire, Burundi, Burkina Faso, and Cameroon have also developed a significant corpus in animation cinema (Colin Dupré). Alassane started his filmmaking career under the supervision of the French filmmaker and ethnographer Jean Rouch in the early 1960s in Niamey, the capital city of Niger. The newly independent Niger created the Institut Nigerien de Recherches en Sciences Sociales (INSS), a social science research institute under the leadership of Jean Rouch. With its audiovisual section, the institute provided on-the-job training for the first generation of Nigerien filmmakers such as Moustapha Alassane, Oumarou Ganda, Inoussa Ousseini, Mariama Hima, and Djingarey Maiga. Alassane directed more than 20 fiction, documentary, and animated films. His cross-over filmography also includes *The Return of an Adventurer* (1966), which is regarded as the first postcolonial African western film. Concerning animation, the 1963 short *La mort de Gandji*, the first sub-Saharan postcolonial animated film, was awarded the Best Short Prize and the Silver Antelope Prize at the World Festival of Black Arts in 1966 in Dakar (Senegal). He later produced other short animated fiction films such as *Bon Voyage Sim* (1966), *Samba the Great* (1978), and *Kokoa* (1985 and 2001). Alassane's animation takes the viewer to a traditional African world of wrestling, heroism, and local practices. In contrast to the other films, *Bon Voyage Sim* stands out as an overtly political production. *Bon Voyage Sim* tells the story of the frog president who returns from an official trip only to be deposed in a military coup. The film's storyline shares similarities with the history of several West African countries, which have known successive military rules from coups: Niger, Nigeria, Burkina Faso, and Mali. In general, animals such as frogs hold a significant place in Alassane's artistic creativity, drawing on the local imaginations about the Niger river that runs through Niamey, the capital city of Niger. The Niger river is the main river in West Africa and the third longest in Africa.

Madagascar: Animation as an Oasis in the Malagasy Cinema Landscape

In addressing the topic of animation and Madagascar, the most likely thing that will instantly cross your interlocutor's mind is Hollywood's animated Madagascar franchise[2] directed by Eric Darnell and Tom McGrath. The first three films in the franchise chronicle the adventures of a number of animals who are attempting to return to New York after escaping the city's zoo and find themselves stranded in Madagascar. Though one might be tempted to guess about any possible linkage between the Madagascar franchise and the island's cinematic practice in animation, which emerged in the 2000s, there does not to appear be any. Madagascar boasts an ever-expanding animation film catalogue such as *Rough Life* (Sitraka Randriamahaly, 2015), *The Bee* (Cid, 2014), *Ray* (Herizo Ramilijaonina, 2012), *Iny Hono Izy Ravorona* (Sitraka Randriamahaly, 2012), *La chasse au lambo* (Sitraka Randriamahaly, 2011), *Selamanana* (Herizo Ramilijaonina, 2010), *Afropower—Afreupouvoir* (Randriamanantsoa Manohiray, 2010), *ILM, Le savoir* (Ridha Andriantomanga, 2008), and *Le soleil se lève ... puis se couche* (Jiva Eric Razafindralambo, 2005).

Animation emerged in the early 2000s as the main cinematic expression in Madagascar, filling the void left by a decades-long lack of significant productions dating back to the 1980s. By the year 2000, some of the well-known Malagasy directors such as Raymond Rajaonarivelo, Benoît Ramampy, and Solo Randrasana had stopped making movies. Auteur cinema suffered from the lack of clearly articulated policies by public authorities to foster sustained productions, which left younger generations of audiovisual storytellers to rely on *débrouillardise* (hustle) by harnessing the potential of new internet-based technologies. Animation seemed the obvious choice for the younger generations, who not only drew on the long tradition of the production of comics on the island, along with geek and manga culture, but also provided an alternate medium of artistic expression given the closure of movie theaters. The emergence of these self-taught and experimental artists has made Madagascar the leading animation producing country in sub-Saharan Africa over the last 15 years, particularly in terms of the relative consistency and number of films released.

As for thematic and aesthetic treatment, rurality appears to be the dominant trait in Malagasy animation, although disparate topics such as World War II veterans depart from the trend of idyllic portrayal of rural Madagascar, scenes of farmers' daily lives, and the tradition of zebu.[3] The aesthetics are built around a timeless rural world and the use of humor. It is worth noting the apparent disconnect between urban and rural life in several animated films. In other words, though the animators are urban artists by residence and upbringing, the city in its complexities is rarely the subject matter of their productions. Does the rural world represent an escape from the harsh city life, or what are the possible explanations for the thematic and aesthetic treatment of rurality? In-depth further research on Malagasy animation is certainly required to provide conclusive answers to these questions.

Though Madagascar boasts of having the most significant and consistent production of animations in sub-Saharan Africa, since the early 2000s, it remains a very fragile and cyclic stream of productions. It is still hard for animators to make a living from their art so they often leave to work in advertisement and communication agencies. As a result, this revolving door impedes sustainability in the production of animations. For instance, from 2013 to 2014, there were no productions because the animators joined advertisement agencies, and the 2017 edition of the film festival 'Rencontres du Film Court' had no animation category in the official competition for lack of submissions. Created by the Malagasy filmmaker Laza and the Institut Français in 2006, the Madagascar-based Rencontres du Film Court is the biggest film festival in the Indian Ocean. The fragility of the animation sector is indicative of the lack of support for the film industry by public authorities. Films are being made only on private initiatives, while the local French cultural center Institut Français and the Rencontres du Film Court offer only two viable dissemination outlets for content producers on the island.

Conclusion

African animation is one of the least-explored genres of African cinema, as scholarly productions are predominantly geared toward live-action films. Yet the animation genre provides untapped insights into the diversity of the continent's cinematic practices. Animation productions have increased significantly from the 63 animated films that the continent had produced by 1993 (Peghini, 2015, 191). Unfortunately, the upturn in production has not been met with equal sustained academic interest because the "discourse on animation from the African continent is scarce, with only a few key scholars directing their attention to sub-Saharan animation artists at large" (Callus, 2010, 58). In this context, a call for more research and scholarly productions on sub-Saharan animation is needed and should be heeded.

Case Study: **Prince Loseno** *(Jean-Michel Kibushi Ndajte Wooto, 2004)*

Animation in Congo and Kibushi's Biography

The history of animation in the Democratic Republic of Congo (DRC)[4] can be traced back to the tradition of comics developed in the 1930s through the publication of daily, weekly, and monthly newspapers such as *L'Echo du Katanga*, *La Croix du Congo*, and *Cosmo-Kin*. These newspapers, as Guido Convents (2014, 27) explains, had sections of comic strips depicting life in the Belgian Congo. The animated series *Les Palabres de Mboloko* (*The Words of Mboloko*), produced between 1953 and 1955 by Roger Jamar and the missionary Alexander Van den Heuvel, are regarded as the first animated films made in the DRC (Convents, 2014, 36). However, Africa was already the subject of Walt Disney animated films such as *Alice Hunting in Africa* (1924), *Alice in the Jungle* (1925), and *Mickey Mouse Jungle Rhythm* (1929), which portrayed Africans stereotypically (Magee, 2012, 129).

Les Palabres de Mboloko is constructed around the protagonist, a dwarf antelope, that outwits fierce and more powerful opponents such as a leopard, a python, and an elephant, and others like a monkey and a tortoise (Convents, 2014, 37).

Jean-Michel Kibushi Ndajte Wooto, the first Congolese animator, was born in 1957, around the time of the production of *Les Palabres de Mboloko*. His works and creative projects brought international attention to animation in the DRC and Central Africa. Unlike most of the self-taught sub-Saharan African animators, Kibushi received formal training in drama and cinema at the National Institute of the Arts in Kinshasa in the 1980s. His Studio Malembe Maa (co)produces his animated films. He has also created the Sankuru Mobile Project, an outreach and educational initiative that screens movies in remote villages in the DRC. So, Kibushi is not only an animator, but also an educator.

In addition to the documentaries *Caravane pour le Sankuru* (2007) and *Roger Jamar et Les Palabres de Mboloko* (2015), Kibushi's animated filmography includes:

- *Le crapaud chez ses beaux-parents* (*The Toad Who Visits His In-Laws*, 1991)
- *Kinshasa, septembre noir* (*Black September in Kinshasa*, 1992)
- *L'orange blanche* (*The White Orange*, 1993)
- *L'éléphant qui pète de la neige* (*The Snow-farting Elephant*, 1993)
- *Muana Mboka* (1996)
- *L'âne et le chat* (*The Donkey and the Cat*, 2001)

- *Première traversée* (*First Crossing*, 2002)
- *Prince Loseno* (2004)
- *Ngando* (2008)

Prince Loseno tells the story of an old king, Mwakana Kasanga Ka Ngolo, on a quest to have an heir to the throne, fearing for the survival of the kingdom after his death. None of his three wives—Otango, Ehola, and Dembo—have given him children, and there is growing anxiety in the king's inner circle that a solution must be found before it is too late. Because "*si le coq ne change pas de poules assez souvent, le poulailler risque de se depeupler* [If the cockerel does not change hens often enough, the chicken pen will soon be empty]" (6:50), according to the king's most influential counselor, Lokoto. So, under the recommendation of the king's first wife, Otango, and Lokoto, the king takes a fourth wife, Dipepe, who is Otango's niece. Prince Loseno is born from their union and ascends to the throne before his father dies. Loseno, meaning "life" in the local language, breathes new life into the kingdom (Figure 5.3).

Preservation of Oral Culture

Jean-Michel Kibushi Ndajte Wooto's approach to the animation medium is that of an artist seeking to preserve the oral storytelling cultures of his people. His animation serves to safeguard oral cultures from extinction.

Figure 5.3 Prince Loseno.

Rapid urbanization, disintegration of traditional communal life because of the influence of "modernity" and capitalist forces, the advent of hand-held electronic devices, and the lack of comprehensive public policies in the culture sector are among the reasons oral stories need more attention. Kibushi may be regarded as an archivist of orality, collecting and storing stories on celluloid or in digital format to preserve the collective memory. So, "he sees his films as a contribution to safeguarding oral stories from his own ethnic group, the Tetela, which he frequently draws on or adapts in his films" (Callus, 2010, 57).

In the larger context of African cinema, the efforts of Kibushi to preserve oral stories or to draw on elements of oral storytelling (proverbs and griot-style narration) fit in with the African cinematic productions of the 1980s on cultural identity[5] and later productions such as *Keïta! The Heritage of the Griot* (Dani Kouyaté, 1995) and *Taafe Fanga* (*Skirt Power*, 1997) by Adama Drabo. With regard to orality in African cinema, Manthia Diawara[6] and Keyan G. Tomaselli[7] demonstrate how elements of oral cultures, such as tales, folk songs, proverbs, dance, and the griot, shape aesthetics and storytelling in African cinema.

Prince Loseno is told in voice-over narration by a griot, played by Kibushi himself. As with most African oral stories, the storyteller starts by setting the story in a distant past and contextualizes it geographically but often with no clear territorial boundaries that would correspond to contemporary African nation-states. This way of introducing the story helps establish its universality, or at least makes it relatable to peoples across many countries despite any cultural specificities.

The film opens on a kingdom sitting above a river. The royal court is standing, demonstrating its height relative to the houses around it. The white background makes the red houses stand out even more to the viewer. The few clouds and early morning fog are clearing, in perfect computer-generated animation, as the sun rises. Simultaneously, we hear the griot announce the story:

> *Voici un royaume lointain au coeur de l'Afrique profonde. Les ancêtres et les vivants y vivent en parfaite harmonie.* [This is a faraway kingdom in the heart of the deepest, darkest Africa. The living and their ancestors live here together in perfect harmony.]

Such film openings in African cinema, in which a griot tells the audience a story or is embedded in the story as griot-character, are common in West African productions such as *Borom Sarret* (Ousmane Sembène, 1963), *Djeli, conte d'aujourd'hui* (Fadika Kramo-Laciné, 1981), *Keïta! The Heritage of the Griot*, and *Taafe Fanga* (*Skirt Power*). The griot plays the role of an omniscient narrator throughout the film by providing background

Figure 5.4 Dipepe is pregnant with Loseno.

information on certain characters. For instance, the viewer learns that the court healer, Mama Yakumba, who routinely performs fertility rituals on the king and his wives, had a romantic relationship with the king when they were both young. That relationship and the prospect of marriage between the two never came to fruition because of palace intrigues, so the disappointment lingers. That is why Mama Yakumba becomes even more vengeful toward the royal court when she is told her services will no longer be needed for the new bride, Dipepe (Figure 5.4).

In addition to the griot-style narration, the extensive use of proverbs throughout the animated film demonstrates how the story is grounded in African oral cultures. The use of proverbs by a speaker shows his/her maturity and wisdom, and in the case of the griot or djeli, mastery of the word. He who masters the word is well regarded in the community and is often called to serve in a leadership position, as is the influential royal counselor, Lokoto. In oral cultures, proverbs, tales, myths, and short stories are all vehicles for production and dissemination of knowledge. Through these elements of orality, one can learn more about a group's cosmogony, philosophical thinking, values, and "*imaginaire collectif*." The meanings of the proverbs in *Prince Loseno* are contextual but also perfectly intelligible outside the limited context of the scenes in which they occur. For example:

> *Les lèvres gâtent les choses, c'est la langue qui répare* [The lips scratch, it's the tongue that mends] (17:42).

General meaning: Opposites work in tandem.

Si la calebasse et la peau arrivent arrivent à cogner, que dire des hommes? [If even gourds and pots can clash with each other, what hope is there for men?] (17:35).

General meaning: Problems or misunderstandings are bound to happen when living together.

Au village des morts, on ne se rend pas en masse, on y va seul [You don't go to the village of the dead in a big crowd, but on your own] (27:05).

General meaning: Death is a personal experience.

La naissance et la mort sont jumelles dans le destin des hommes. Tombe le bananier, pousse le bourgeon [Life and death are intertwined in the destiny of man. The banana tree falls, the bud sprouts] (27:35).

General meaning: Life and death are inseparable.

For orality and cinema, the larger question or debate raised by Kibushi's animated films, and by live-action films by many African directors, is the appropriateness or challenges of the film medium in preserving oral cultures that are not fixed expressive forms. In other words, does the recording of oral stories on a fixed format such as celluloid or digital risk changing the nature of such stories and how they are performed? What does the transfer of orality to recorded audiovisual materials mean for the preservation of African cultures? However, the two forms of storytelling do not have to be examined in oppositional terms. Film could be regarded as a continuum of that orality, as it adds another layer and dimension to oral storytelling.

Notes

1 Manthia Diawara refers to a corpus of African films that focuses on African culture and history against the backdrop of local societies that are fragmented by the multiple effects of colonization (140).

2 *Madagascar* (2005), *Madagascar: Escape 2 Africa* (2008), *Madagascar: Europe's Most Wanted* (2012), and *Penguins of Madagascar* (2014).

3 A species of cattle that is used for work, sacrificial ceremonies, and entertainment events (zebu wrestling). It represents one of the cultural and identity symbols of Madagascar.

4 Formerly Belgian Congo, then Zaïre when it gained its political independence in 1960. The country has been known as the DRC since May 1997.

5 *Djeli, conte d'aujourd'hui* (Fadika Kramo-Laciné, 1981) and *Wend Kuuni* (Gaston Kaboré, 1982).

6 "Popular Culture and Oral Traditions in African Film."

7 "Towards a Theory of Orality in African Cinema."

Bibliography and Filmography

Animation et création: univers du cinéma de Moustapha Alassane. Dir. Debra Boyd-Buggs. Culture Encounters, 2002.

Bendazzi, Ginnalberto. "African Cinema Animation." *Enter Text* 4, no. 1 (2004): 10–26.

Bon Voyage Sim. Dir. Moustapha Alassane. P.O.M Films, 2009.

Bordwell, David, and Kristin Thompson. *Film Art: An Introduction*. 10th ed. New York: McGraw-Hill, 2012.

Callus, Paula. "Animation as a Socio-political Commentary: An Analysis of the Animated Films of Congolese Director Jean Michel Kibushi." *Journal of African Media Studies* 2, no. 1 (2010): 55–71.

Callus, Paula. "Animation, Fabrication, Photography: Reflections upon the Intersecting Practices of Sub-Saharan Artists within the Moving Image." *African Arts* 48, no. 3 (2015): 58–69.

Convents, Guido. *Images & Animation. Le Cinéma d'animation en Afrique Centrale*. Kessel Lo, Belgium: Afrika Filmfestival and SIGNIS, 2014.

Diawara, Manthia. *African Cinema: Politics and Culture*. Bloomington: Indiana University Press, 1992.

Diawara, Manthia. "Popular Culture and Oral Traditions in African Film." *Film Quarterly* 41, no. 3 (Spring 1988): 6–14.

Dupré, Colin. *Cinéma malgache: la renaissance passé par l'animation*. www.inaglobal .fr/cinema/article/cinema-malgache-la-renaissance-passe-par-l-animation-8197. Accessed 5/21/2017.

Kokoa. Dir. Moustapha Alassane. Tahoua Productions, 2001. 14 minutes. Animation.

L'Afrique s'anime. P.O.M. Films, 2009.

La mort du Gandji. Dir. Moustapha Alassane. P.O.M Films, 2009.

Moustapha Alassane, cineaste du possible. Dir. Christian Lelong and Maria Silvia Bazzoli. Harmattan vidéo, 2008.

Peghini, Julie. Review of Guido Convents. Images et animation. Le Cinéma d'animation en Afrique centrale. Introduction au cinéma d'animation en République démocratique du Congo, au Rwanda et au Burundi. Kessel-Lo / Leuven: Afrika Filmfestival, 2014. *Études Littéraires Africaines* 39 (2015): 190–192.

Tomaselli, G. Keyan. "Towards a Theory of Orality in African Cinema." *Research in African Literatures* 26, no. 3 (1995): 18–35.

Suggested Readings and Films

Barlet, Oliver. "Cinéma d'animation: une nouvelle écriture." *Africultures* 22 (November 1999): 51–52.

Bazzoli, Maria Sylvia. *African cartoon: il cinema di animazione in Africa*. Milan: Il Castoro, 2003.

Blanchon, Karine. *Les cinémas de Madagascar, 1937–2007*. Paris: Harmattan, 2010.

Callus, Paula. "Animation as a Socio-political Commentary: An Analysis of the Animated Films of Congolese Director Jean Michel Kibushi." *Journal of African Media Studies* 2, no. 1 (2010): 55–71.

Callus, Paula. "Reading Animation through the Eyes of Anthropology: A Case Study of Sub-Saharan African Animation." *Animation* 7, no. 2 (2012): 113–130.

Dobson, Nichola, Annabelle Honess Roe, Amy Ratelle, and Caroline Ruddell. *The Animation Studies Reader*. London and New York: Bloomsbury Academic, 2018.

Documentary Educational Resources. *Jean-Michel Kibushi: Palabres animés du griot*. Watertown: Documentary Educational Resources, 2017.

Furniss, Maureen. *Art in Motion: Animation Aesthetics*. New Barnet: John Libbey Publishing, 2008.

Johnston, Ollie, and Frank Thomas. *The Illusion of Life: Disney Animation*. New York: Disney Editions, 1995.

Haffner, Pierre. *Palabres sur le cinématographe: Initiation au cinéma*. Kinshasa, Zaïre: Presses africaines, 1978.

Kolosary Cinéma Malgasy. Paris: Institut Français, 2016.

Magee, L. Carol. *Africa in the American Imagination: Popular Culture and Racialized Identities and African Visual Culture*. Jackson: University Press of Mississippi, 2012.

Ramirez, Christian, and Francis Rolot. *Histoire du cinéma colonial au Zaïre, Rwanda et au Burundi*. Tervuren: Musée royal de l'Afrique centrale, 1985.

Ward, Paul. "Some Thoughts on Theory–Practice Relationships in Animation Studies." *Animation: An Interdisciplinary Journal* 1, no. 2 (2006): 229–245.

Wells, Paul. "The Beautiful Village and the True Village." *Art and Design Profile* 12, no. 53 (1997): 40–46.

Wells, Paul. *Understanding Animation*. New York: Routledge, 1998.

6   Introductory Study of African Film Scores

Have you ever once stopped to reflect on:

- The functions of music in film?
- The impactful experience that diegetic and non-diegetic music have on you as a viewer?
- The typology of music uses in African cinema?
- The similarities and dissimilarities between African cinema and Western cinema in their deployment of music?

This chapter not only addresses these four questions, but also serves as one of the first introductions to a relatively unexplored topic in the academic field of African cinema.

Only a few scholars have produced works on the subject, such as those of Françoise Pfaff, Alexander Fisher, and Sheila Petty.[1] This chapter builds on the works by these three scholars by proposing a typology of diegetic African film music: griot performances, embedded entertainment, ritual performances, music-themed narrative films, and the musical film genre. The case study on *Black Girl* (Ousmane Sembène, 1966) focuses on the space and time dimensions of non-diegetic music. Diegetic music is defined as music that has its source within the film's world (for example, on-screen performances) such as in *The Wizard of Oz* (Victor Fleming, 1939), *West Side Story* (Jerome Robbins and Robert Wise, 1961), and *Dreamgirls* (Bill Condon, 2006). On the other hand, non-diegetic music is edited in during postproduction and is often the work of renowned composers like Philip Glass, Hans Zimmer, Danny Elfman, and Alexandre Desplat.

Film music is an aesthetic and creative tool that is critical in both shaping the viewer's experience of the story and adding layers of meaning to the storytelling. One of the powers of film sound is how the blending of image and sound affects the viewer's experience (e.g.,

DOI: 10.4324/9781003246763-8

horror movies). But most important is how music can convey particular meaning or symbolic value to the image, which could have otherwise escaped the viewer. In other words, film sound provides a symbiotic relationship between music and image in a perfect meaning-making stylistic approach, which Claudia Gorbman refers to as "mutual implication" in her widely acclaimed book, *Unheard Melodies: Narrative Film Music* (1987). African cinema emphasizes time and space dimensions, directing the viewer's attention to a particular scene, creating suspense, and heightening expectation. Thus, it showcases different usages of what is called diegetic and non-diegetic music. The Senegalese musician Wasis Diop is, by far, the best-known West African film score composer of the last 20 years. Examples of films that Wasis Diop has composed for are provided later in the chapter. Whether it is diegetic or non-diegetic, music is omnipresent in sub-Saharan African films in different variations, which are examined in this chapter. Music is integral to sub-Saharan African cinema because it permeates the actual social life of communities, ranging from joyous celebrations (weddings and baptisms), to sacred ceremonies in royal courts, to ritual performances accompanying funeral ceremonies.

Diegetic Music in African Cinema

Diegetic music is deployed in several ways in African cinema that can be grouped into five main categories: griot performances, embedded entertainment, ritual performances, music-themed narrative films, and the musical film genre. These different uses of diegetic music underline the diversity and frequency of on-screen music performance in African cinema.

The griot is a central figure in the oral tradition, as she/he is charged with passing down the history of the community through songs, short stories, or praises. As a result, "the figure of the griot, symbol of the tradition, has also been often represented in African films" (Diawara, 1988, 9). In these representations of the griot in African cinema, the emphasis is very often placed on his/her role as an entertainer and educator, thrusting the filmmaker into the role of a contemporary griot storyteller. Performances by griots in many African films range from singing praises of characters' lineages to live instrumental music entertainment of audiences through kora music. In Sembène Ousmane's short film *Borom Sarret* (1963) and last movie[2] *Moolaadé* (2004), for instance, the director gives two different portrayals of the griot figure, showcasing his/her oratory skills in an (un) ethical way. The griot, master of the word, can be a positive or negative force in society. The well-dressed griot in *Borom Sarret* extracted the little money the cart driver had by lauding the high deeds of his lineage. However, Ousmane Sembène gives a different portrayal of the griot figure through the griotte[3] character, Sana, in *Moolaadé* as the motivator-in-chief in the fight to end female genital mutilation, as shown in the closing scene in which she accompanies the protagonist, Collé Ardo, to confront the village elders. In both portrayals of the griot, mastery of oratory skills and a deep knowledge of collective history make their praise-singing in the local languages more entertaining to both on-screen characters and culturally competent viewers than just a regular musical soundtrack.

   The entertaining function of the griot is also highlighted through music performance within films in front of an audience. The opening scene of the Malian director Adama Drabo's *Taafe Fanga* (*Skirt Power*, 1997) shows an elegantly dressed griot coming out of his house one evening to perform for an audience that has gathered in the large compound. The griot starts playing the kora when a young woman arriving late creates some chaos in the crowd because she wants to join the men's group instead of sitting with the women, which is in defiance of local customs. This incident provides the starting point of the story's narrative arc, thus underlining the narrative function of the griot as an "expository device [...] used to convey information about the plot" (Pfaff, 1984, 62). Contrary to the opening musical performance by the griot as a narrative device, such as that in *Taafe Fanga*, other griot music performances in African cinema are placed strategically in relief scenes to regulate mounting tensions among characters. This can be seen in *Karmen Geï* (2001), by the Senegalese filmmaker Joseph Gaï Ramaka, in the scene in which the prison warden, Angelique, pleads her case to Karmen's mother on the beach. Angelique is deeply in love with the free-spirited protagonist, Karmen, who seems to care less about their relationship since her release from the women's island prison off the coast of Dakar. Angelique's emotional distress is palpable in the scene, drawing the viewer's empathy for her. In a reverse shot, the director shows a griotte, played by the famous Senegalese singer Yandé Codou Sène, singing to the sea about the pain of losing a loved one. Her singing not only enhances the dramatic effect but also provides some release for a particularly emotionally charged scene. Thus, "music is an emotional punctuation which stimulates imagination. It may create or stress mood, announce events, and help to build dramatic tension" (Pfaff, 1984, 65). What is critical to observe in the use of griot performances in African cinema is how the griot smoothly navigates between the different roles of omniscient narrator, narrator-character, and entertainer.

   In addition to griot performances, other forms of diegetic music are embedded in the construction of African audiovisual stories, including on-screen performances by characters or the use of props such as stereos. Radio sets not only allow characters to entertain themselves through music, but also contribute to deepening the viewer's experience of the film's music or soundtrack. In her essay "The Remediation of Radio in African Cinema: *Life on Earth* and *Moolaade*" (2017), Marissa J. Moorman demonstrates how acoustics may be regarded as a major component of the African filmmaking sensibility. In certain African films, the record player serves as a means of negotiation by bringing opponents together for reconciliation. For instance, in the war drama film *Camp de Thiaroye* (Sembène Ousmane, 1998), featuring the demobilization of African veterans of World War II who fought alongside French troops, the reconciliation scene between the Senegalese Sergeant Diatta and the American GI is centered on the two listening to jazz music on a turntable record player. Thus, "through their mutual love of jazz (a musical idiom with its roots in the African-American experience), the soldiers find a rapport and commonality that transcends their national allegiances" (Fisher, 2009, 198). Similar examples in African cinema include *Xala* (Sembène Ousmane, 1975), which opens with a group of dancers performing to live music; multiple live performances by the Congolese musicians Papa Wemba and Pepe Kalé in *La vie est rose* (*Life Is Rosy;* Mweze Ngangura, 1987); the South African road trip comedy *Bunny Chow* (John Barker, 2006) that takes the protagonists to the rock festival Oppikoppi; and Burkinabe director Boubakar Diallo's drama comedy *Sofia* (2004), which received the Best Music award at the Africa Movie Academy Awards in Lagos, Nigeria. This film made especially good use of the talent and performance of the Burkinabe musician Bill Aka Kora.

Diegetic music is also deployed in African films as the main narrative structure and the focus of the thematic treatment. Musicals and music-themed narrative films represent a sizable segment of productions such as *Karmen Geï*, *La vie est rose*, and *Bal poussière* (*Dancing in the Dust*) by the Ivorian director Henri Duparc (1988), and the critically acclaimed *Félicité* by the Senegalese filmmaker Alain Gomis (2016).

Karmen Geï is an African adaptation of the novella *Carmen* by the 19th-century French writer Prosper Mérimée. The novella has been the subject of many cinematic and operatic interpretations, including the opera by the French composer Georges Bizet and the African American musical film version *Carmen Jones* (Otto Preminger, 1954). *Karmen Geï* features performances by the renowned Doudou Ndiaye Rose's band of 50 drummers, and songs by the Senegalese singers El Hadj Ndiaye and Yandé Codou Sène. *Karmen Geï* draws on the local musical practices of the *sabar*, *mbalax*, and griot songs. *La vie est rose* and *Félicité* take the viewer on the journeys of two aspiring musicians in Kinshasa, a city known throughout Africa as a music and trendsetting hub until the end of the 1990s when Côte d'Ivoire and Nigeria emerged as major players on the music scene. In *La vie est rose*, the protagonist, Kourou, leaves his village to pursue a music career in Kinshasa where he will have to be resourceful and resilient in his efforts to realize his dream. Resilience is also evident in *Félicité*, as the bar-singer protagonist races against time to find money for her son's leg surgery. The relationship between music and personal resilience is thoroughly examined in *Life Is Rosy* and *Félicité*. Both films show how the pursuit of music as a creative passion or career path gives the individual the mental and emotional strength to overcome obstacles. Thus, music becomes a source of resilience in the face of hardship. In addition, music could also be regarded as a means to bring about social change or to combat injustice in oppressive political regimes. In this regard, Fela Anikulapo Kuti, the icon of the Afrobeat music genre from the 1970s through the 1990s, used music as a "weapon" to fight corruption and injustice under the military regimes in Nigeria. As dissenting voices are silenced through imprisonments or extrajudicial killings, the music of Fela Kuti became a rallying call to the masses to be resilient and resist the human rights violations committed by military regimes. The Ivorian reggae music stars Alpha Blondy and Tiken Jah Fakoly are also known for using music to raise political awareness and motivate people to withstand the hardships of everyday life. So, there is a well-established connection between music and resilience.[4]

Non-diegetic Music

According to the scholar Alexander Fisher, African film's frequent use of diegetic music stands in sharp contrast to classical Hollywood movies' reliance on non-diegetic music. The generalizing nature of Fisher's assertion may be misleading, given the creative uses of non-diegetic sound in Nollywood-style productions.[5] However, the merit of Fisher's statement resides in the fact that it points out a noticeable trend beyond non-diegetic music in African auteur cinema. This situation is further demonstrated by the limited number of established African film composers, particularly evident in francophone West and Central Africa. The Senegalese musician Wasis Diop remains the most well-known sub-Saharan African film music composer. His compatriot Ismaël Lô is a less well-known film soundtrack composer. Wasis Diop, the younger brother of the Senegalese filmmaker Djibril Mambety Diop, has composed the soundtracks to more than 20 films, most by West African directors. Wasis developed a musical style that blends folklore, jazz, and modern pop, which has the potential to provide a local context for the narratives, build their universal appeal, and enhance the film's overall dramatic effect. Such is the case with Diop's emotionally charged scoring of *Delwende* (Pierre Yaméogo, 2005), as elderly women are being falsely accused of witchcraft and persecuted from their villages to Ouagadougou where they are welcomed in a shelter. Wasis Diop's extensive film scoring experience includes scores for *Africa Paradis* (Sylvestre Amoussou, 2006) and *Indochina: Traces of a Mother* (Idrissou Mora-Kpai, 2011), both from Benin; *Samba Traore* (Idrissa Ouedraogo, 1992) and *Waiting for the Vote* (Missa Hebié, 2011) from Burkina Faso; *Daratt* (*Dry Season*, 2006), *Un homme qui crie* (*A Screaming Man*, 2010), and *A Season in France* (2017) by Mahamat Saleh Haroun from Chad; *TGV* (Moussa Touré, 1998), *Hyènes* (*Hyenas*, 1992), and *La Petite Vendeuse de Soleil* (*The Little Girl Who Sold the Sun*, 1999) by Djibril Mambety Diop from Senegal.

The Cameroonian Manu Dibango is the other major African film music composer who has consistently produced quality scoring since composing the soundtrack to *Ceddo* (Sembène Ousmane, 1977). Like Wasis Diop, Dibango's music is a fusion drawing on different genres such as traditional Makossa music, jazz, Afrobeat, and African rumba. Dibango has scored music for more than 20 films (TV series, feature-length films, and documentaries), including *Kirikou découvre les animaux d'Afrique* (Jean-François Bordier, 2007), *Kirikou and the Wild Beasts* (Bénédicte Galup and Michel Ocelot, 2005), *Hollow City* (Maria João Ganga, 2004), *September 11* (segment "Burkina Faso"; Idrissa Ouedraogo, 2002), and *How to Make Love to a Negro without Getting Tired* (Jacques W. Benoit, 1989). The other Senegalese musician Ismaël Lô is credited for his scoring of *Yayoma* (Lluís Danés, 2012), *All about My Mother* (Pedro Almodóvar, 1999), and *Afrique, mon Afrique …* (Idrissa Ouedraogo, 1995).

In addition to non-diegetic music composed by renowned African musicians for African auteur cinema, different sound designs and creative uses of music are also evident in the popular Nigerian and Ghanaian home or video movies. Video and digital technological innovation has opened up possibilities for Nigerian and Ghanaian audiovisual storytellers to manipulate sound in creative ways, particularly in constructing a world filled with supernatural beings or occult forces. In analyzing the technological dimensions of the Ghanaian ghost movie, Carmela Garritano demonstrates how the visual and aural effects of the ghost's (re)appearance are rendered through the use of computer-generated effects. In *Suzzy* (Veronica Cudjoe, 1993), for instance, "the musical motif that accompanied the ghost's appearance […] was a simple tune created with an electronic keyboard" (2017, 204). *The Chase* (Jon Gil, 2011), the first Ghanaian slasher movie, showcases a more advanced use of digital sound through "sharp and synthetic diegetic sounds as well as computer-generated ripping, dragging, and screeching" (2017, 205). If Nollywood and Ghallywood productions, as a new cinematic practice within African cinema, have attracted scholarly attention over the last 15 years, their sonic and musical dimensions remain largely unexplored.

Case Study: Non-diegetic Music—Space and Time Dimensions of Film Music in *La Noire de* … (*Black Girl*) (Ousmane Sembène, 1966)

La Noire de … (*Black Girl*), an African cinema classic, is regarded as the first sub-Saharan African film to gain international recognition, as demonstrated by the three major awards the film received in 1966: the Jean Vigo Prize in France, Best Feature at the Festival of Black Arts in Dakar, and the Golden Tanit at the Carthage Film Festival. Part of the attraction of *La Noire de* … resides in the aesthetic choices made to build the opposition between agency and voicelessness throughout the film. In this regard, the voice-over stands out as a marker of the protagonist Diouana's lack of control over her social environment in France, which is marked by domestic servitude. This well-constructed and emotionally charged voice-over narration has certainly contributed to making *Black Girl* an engaging film and, most importantly, an object of continued aesthetic inquiry. The use of music, to complement or to contrast with the voice-over, underlines the noticeable ways in which space and time are conveyed on the screen to depict Diouana's life trajectory from relative freedom in Dakar to exploitation as a maid on the French Riviera. The film features three different kinds of music to strategically construct and delineate instances of alienation and happiness, but also to locate the unfolding drama in the context of time. How does music work in the film to contrast Dakar and the French Riviera by conveying spatial openness and confinement? What is the historical and aesthetic significance of the use of non-diegetic, off-screen music in *La Noire de* …? By reading the African classic *Black Girl* through the lens of film music, we can better understand some of the aesthetic approaches to African cinema.

Drawing on Bordwell's space and time dimensions in film,[6] we can see how the music in *La Noire de* … is deployed in numerous ways to contextualize the story spatially, denote the expression of past versus present, and shape the viewer's understanding of the image. The voice-over narration in *La Noire de* … is a very effective means of articulating oppression and the imbalance in power relationships at the individual and state levels. The voice-over artfully conveys the pervasive sense of exploitation and powerlessness, which the protagonist embodies, as well as the unfolding human suffering and trauma of alienation in France.

Besides the voice-over, the musical rendering of oppression is particularly poignant through the use of three different kinds of scores: African instrumental music; European instrumental music that accompanies the scenes set solely in France, where the protagonist is voiceless; and African vocal music that accompanies scenes set in Dakar to highlight Diouana's empowerment. These music scores are perfectly aligned with the spatial and temporal constructions of exclusion in the film.

In general, isolation in the film is depicted as a binary opposition, such as indoor versus outdoor, Dakar versus French Riviera, and mobility versus restriction. The three kinds of music scores provide spatial and temporal markers in the narrative structure, reflecting Diouana's freedom of movement in Dakar in opposition to her physical and emotional confinement in France. Nowhere is this more evident than the scene in which Diouana is shown frustrated after being told by Madame not to take offense at the racist behavior of a guest who wanted to kiss Diouana because he had never kissed a black woman before. Ousmane Sembène uses the flashback technique to contrast Diouana's current situation with her past life in Dakar. The end of the flashback shows Diouana taking three children out to play as fast-paced African vocal music plays in the background. The music is performed by a griot as a hymn to the bravery of the historical figure Kelefa Sanneh,[7] which draws a parallel to Diouana's struggle in life. Then, the camera quickly cuts to a medium shot of a pensive Diouana sitting on her bed as melancholic African instrumental music plays. A quick B-roll transition shot with piano music provides the soundtrack to a high-angle framing of Diouana cleaning the kitchen, then an interlude with low-tempo instrumental African music. So, in less than two minutes of runtime, this sequence showcases a meaningful blending of three music scores to signal shifts in space and time. In addition, the slow and steady tempos of both the African and European instrumental scores accompanying the scenes set in France greatly enhance the dramatic and emotional effects of the story on the viewer because the unfolding drama is dragging out, with no apparent end in sight. Similar use of music is evident throughout the film, such as the disenchantment scene in which another flashback takes the protagonist back to the good old days in Dakar when she was still dating Mamadou.

African music carries an identity marker as well as a symbolic value related to how much screen time the protagonist gets. There is a strong correlation between the on-screen characters and the music being played in *Black Girl*, which is particularly true for the character of Diouana. For instance, only twice in the entire film is African music played while Diouana is on screen with another character, and that happens only in common areas of the apartment, particularly in the living room. The first time is when the little boy, Philip, asks Diouana whether they can play together, and the second time happens when Monsieur gives Diouana money for her salary, which he had never bothered to pay until then. This differentiated use of music adds another layer of meaning to the filmic construction of space and time that denotes the various ways "music identifies groups of people, geographical areas, and historical periods and evokes atmospheres" (Pfaff, 1984, 67). Music and image mutually imply meaning, so music should not be just a generic accompaniment to the image, as is the case in certain Hollywood blockbuster movies such as *Independence Day* (Roland Emmerich, 1996), in which the music score is played throughout the entire movie. African cinema provides examples of music/image implication that carry great significance regarding the representation of space and time, as seen in the case of *Black Girl*.

The strategic use of various types of music scores to accentuate the thematic treatment of oppression in *La Noire de …* provides an additional entry point into this African film classic beyond the usual reference to the effective use of voice-over or the historical significance as the first sub-Saharan African film to gain international recognition. Whether the music is instrumental or vocal, its differentiated use is based on space and time, adding a layer of meaning to the oppositional representation of the open, populous Dakar versus the secluded and lonely apartment in France. The numerous flashbacks made against the backdrop of Diouana's current situation take on a far greater meaning with the inclusion of the slow-paced and steady instrumental soundtrack. The convergence of aesthetics and thematic treatment here provides insights into the film's artistry. Plainly, those insights are music/image relationships and meaning. This makes African cinema an important site for investigating the implication of music and image.

Notes

1 Pfaff's book chapter on "The Africanness of Sembène's Film Language" (43–82), Fisher's articles "Vocal Spaces and Oral Traces: Voice-Over, Orality, and Ousmane Sembène's Early Post-colonial Critique" and "Music, Magic, and the Mythic: The Dynamics of Visual and Aural Discourse in Souleymane Cissé's *Yeelen*," and "The Rise of the African Musical: Postcolonial Disjunction in *Karmen Geï* and *Madame Brouette*," by Sheila Petty.

2 The director passed away in 2007 at the age of 84.

3 Female griot.

4 In the United States, the history of blues shows how this musical form/style originated as a way for slaves to find strength in themselves while working in inhuman conditions on the plantations.

5 Popular cinema: small-budget video-movies made by mostly self-taught audio-visual storytellers.
6 In the tenth edition of *Film Art: An Introduction*, Bordwell and Thompson note four dimensions of film sound: rhythm, fidelity, space, and time (281–298).
7 A 19th-century Senegambian warrior prince whose heroism is recounted by griots in a variety of songs.

Bibliography and Filmography

Borom Sarret. Dir. Ousmane Sembène. New Yorker Video, 2005.

Camp de Thiaroye. Dir. Ousmane Sembène. New Yorker Video, 1998.

Diawara, Manthia. "Popular Culture and Oral Traditions in African Film." *Film Quarterly* 41, no. 3 (1988): 6–14.

Fisher, Alexander. "Med Hondo's *Sarraounia*: The Musical Articulation of Cultural Transformation." *Music, Sound, and the Moving Image* 3, no. 2 (Autumn 2009): 195–213.

Fisher, Alexander. "Modes of Griot Inscription in African Cinema." *Journal of African Media Studies* 8, no. 1 (2016): 5–16.

Fisher, Alexander. "Music, Magic, and the Mythic: The Dynamics of Visual and Aural Discourse in Souleymane Cissé's *Yeelen*." *CINEJ Cinema Journal* 2, no. 1 (2012): 1–18.

Fisher, Alexander. "Vocal Spaces and Oral Traces: Voice-over, Orality, and Ousmane Sembene's Early Post-colonial Critique." In *Locating the Voice in Film*, ed. Tom Whittaker and Sarah Wright, 209–225. New York: Oxford University Press, 2016.

Garritano, Carmela. "The Materiality of Genre: Analog and Digital Ghosts in Video Movies from Ghana." *The Cambridge Journal of Postcolonial Literary Inquiry* 4, no. 2 (2017): 191–206.

Gorbman, Claudia. *Unheard Melodies: Narrative Film Music*. London: British Film Institute, 1987.

Karmen Geï. Dir. Joseph Ramaka Gaï. Kino, 2005.

La vie est belle (Life Is Rosy). Dir. Mweze Ngangura and Benoît Lamy. California Newsreel, 1987.

Moolaade. Dir. Ousmane Sembène. Kino, 2016.

Moorman, Marissa. J. "The Remediation of Radio in African Cinema: *Life on Earth* and *Moolaade*." *Cinema Journal* 57, no. 1 (Fall 2017): 94–116.

Pfaff, Françoise. *The Cinema of Ousmane Sembène: A Pioneer of African Film*. Westport: Greenwood, 1984.

Sofia. Dir. Boubakar Diallo. Les Films du drommadaire, 2004.

Taafe Fanga (Skirt Power). Dir. Adama Drabo. California Newsreel, 2008.

Suggested Readings and Films

Adorno, W. Theodor, and Hanns Eisler. *Composing for the Films*. London and New York: Bloomsbury Academic, 2007.

Altman, Rick, ed. *Sound Theory, Sound Practice*. New York: Routledge, 1992.

Chernoff, John Miller. *African Rhythm and African Sensibility: Aesthetics and Social Action in African Musical Idioms*. Chicago: University of Chicago Press, 1981.

Dovey, Lindiwe, and Angela Impey. "Sound, Politics, and Pleasure in Early 'Black' South African Cinema." *Journal of African Cultural Studies* 22, no. 1 (2010): 57–73.

Félicité. Dir. Alain Gomis. Jour2fête, 2017.

Faulkner, Robert. R. *Hollywood Studio Musicians: Their Work and Careers in the Recording Industry*. New Brunswick: Transaction, 2013.

Faulkner, Robert. R. *Music on Demand: Composers and Careers in the Hollywood Film Industry*. New Brunswick: Transaction, 2008.

Gorbman, Claudia. *Unheard Melodies: Narrative Film Music*. London: British Film Institute, 1987.

Letcher, Christopher. "Mbaqanga, Bollywood and Beethoven on the Beachfront: A Composer's Perspective on Representation and Identity in the Film *My Black Little Heart*." *Ethnomusicology Forum* 18, no. 1 (June 2009): 21–36.

Petty, Sheila. "The Rise of the African Musical: Postcolonial Disjunction in *Karmen Geï* and *Madame Brouette*." *Journal of African Cinemas* 1, no. 1 (2009): 95–112.

Pfaff, Françoise. *The Cinema of Ousmane Sembène: A Pioneer of African Film*. Westport: Greenwood, 1984.

Slobin, Mark, ed. *Global Soundtracks: Worlds of Film Music*. Middletown: Wesleyan University Press, 2008.

Stone, Ruth M. *Music in West Africa: Experiencing Music, Expressing Culture*. Oxford and New York: Oxford University Press, 2005.

Part III
African Film Criticism

7 Critical Reading Lenses in the Study of African Cinemas

As there are different traditions and practices in African cinema, there also exist several critical lenses through which to read African cinema. The multiplicity of critical tools is evidenced in the existing scholarly contributions on African cinema that draw on different frameworks such as film history (Paulin Soumanou Vieyra, James M. Burns, and James E. Genova), psychoanalysis (Kenneth Harrow and David Murphy), gender (Sheila Petty and Beti Ellerson), postcolonial theory (Olivier Barlet, Kenneth Harrow, and Akin Adesokan), Third Cinema and Marxist (Teshome Gabriel), cultural politics (Férid Boughedir, Manthia Diawara, and Frank N. Ukadike), and the African film industry and its global positionality (John Haynes, Martin Mhando, Alessandro Jedlowski, and Moradewun Adejunmobi). These reading lenses should not be considered as mutually exclusive because they can be presented in combination with each other, nor should one assume that these scholars are indefinitely tethered to a particular critical apparatus. The common denominator among all these theoretical approaches resides in their analytical approach to film as text—textual analysis, that is, the idea that a film can be read on the merits of its formal elements. In other words, meanings can be made out of films by interpreting them without prior knowledge of the director's biography, for instance. In this respect, a film is read as an object independent from directors' lives, although the formal training and ideological leanings of certain African filmmakers (such as Ousmane Sembène and Med Hondo) or historical circumstances of production are often referenced in the analysis of their work by scholars. So, these different critical frameworks should be understood as grounded in textual interpretation, which is by far the dominant mode of analysis in the scholarship on African cinema. The critical frameworks presented in this chapter should not be taken as fixed, immutable categories but rather as fluid structures that may be organized differently by various scholars. Instead, they are offered

DOI: 10.4324/9781003246763-10

as guidelines and possible lines of investigation, among so many others. For this introduction to the critical readings of African cinema, the postcolonial, global positionality, gender, and industry frameworks are selected to serve as case studies, with the emerging trends in the theorization of African cinema as a conclusion to the chapter.

The Postcolonial Critical Framework

Besides serving to understand cinema, postcolonial theory has been widely used in the reading of African postcolonial literature and cultures (*The Empire Writes Back*, 2002), and history and politics in the postcolony (*On the Postcolony*, 2001). As a definition,

> Postcolonialism involves first all the argument that the nations of the three non-western continents (Africa, Asia, Latin America) are largely in a situation of subordination to Europe and North America, and in a position of economic inequality. Postcolonialism names a politics and philosophy of activism that contests that disparity, and so continues in a new way the anti-colonial struggles of the past.
>
> (Young, 2003, 4)

In addition, Young notes that there is "no single entity called postcolonial theory: postcolonialism, as a term, describes practices and ideas as various as those within feminism or socialism" (2003, 7). In African cinema, several reading lenses or paradigms are grouped under this encompassing framework to underline numerous ways of making sense of African cinematic productions in the post-independence era. In the immediate aftermath of political liberation from colonial subjugation, the newfound voices in audiovisual storytelling carry the mission of decolonizing the gaze and nation-building, which presents similarities with the Third Cinema movement of the 1960s and 1970s. "Decolonizing the gaze" is a term used by the African cinema scholar Olivier Barlet to refer to the shift in enunciation and perspective whereby African stories and images are presented by Africans themselves, as they took possession of the film medium in the wake of political independence gained from colonial powers. By moving in front of the camera as subjects (with limited agency in the construction of their own stories) to behind the camera as directors, Africans would be in a better position to rewrite their own history and correct the distorted representations of culture and people that colonial cinema exhibits. In this respect, deconstructive criticism is often deployed to contextualize the politico-historical significance of the birth of African cinema and to underline the role of cinema in helping

Africans reclaim their history, culture, and identity. There is a need "to dispel these outmoded and untenable myths which permeate the interpretation of African history, culture and now cinema, of how Africa is seen as a cinematographic desert, a filmic cul-de-sac" (Ukadike, 2014, 3). The cinematic deconstruction of colonial legacy has sometimes taken the form of what Manthia Diawara refers to as the "return to the sources" films (1992, 140)—a filmic corpus of the 1980s and 1990s that addresses identity and cultural emancipation such as *Wend Kuuni* (*God's Gift*, 1982) by the Burkinabe director Gaston Kaboré, *Keita, l'héritage du griot* (*Keita, Heritage of the Griot*, 1995) by the Burkinabe director Dani Kouyaté, or *Pièces d'identité* (*Identity Pieces*, 1998) by Congolese filmmaker Mweze Ngangura. So, whether it is decolonizing the gaze by (re)appropriating the film medium or deconstructing homogenizing portrayals of Africa by the West, pan-Africanist themes and anti-colonial rhetoric make up some of the most recurrent features in that scholarship.

As for the nation-building paradigm, it is premised on the idea of film being used as a means for political and cultural liberation to better foster the development of the 'young' nation-states following the end of colonial rule. It also concerns the critique of postcolonial African political elites. Concretely, cinema serves as a didactic tool to help develop conscious awareness of the masses with regard to questions of socioeconomic development. This pedagogical dimension of African cinema is echoed in Ousmane Sembène's often-cited likening of African cinema to "the evening school of the masses" who lack Western-style education. Film, as an image-driven narrative medium, would be a perfect vehicle to educate the masses. Established in 1969, the Pan-African Federation of Filmmakers (FEPACI) decided at its 1975 meeting in Algiers to actively participate in the anti-imperialist fight on the continent by making politically committed films. In this context, the emphasis is on the instructional values of films over their commercial values (Diawara, 1996, 103). Cultural emancipation of the newly independent African nation-states also meant some degree of control over the distribution circuit of the cultural industry in each country. The prevailing situation at that time was that after a decade of political independence, the screen media landscape in the vast majority of African countries was still marked by the monopolistic position of Western companies such as Monegasque companies SECMA and COMACICO, and the Motion Pictures Export Association of America (Boughedir, 1996, 115). These business entities dominated the distribution circuit from film imports to operations of movie theaters in Africa. To remedy this situation, FEPACI adopted the "Niamey Manifesto" in 1982 to encourage the emergence of local cultural industries—through different economic models ranging from nationalizations to the creation of joint ventures. These initiatives by FEPACI should be understood in the context of cultural nationalism where assertive sovereignty over identity and culture is prominent. Though African cinema has evolved from the rhetoric of nation-building and cultural nationalism that characterized the first two decades of its history, it may be important to note that "to this day didacticism remains a central strand in francophone filmmaking" (Şaul, 2010, 133). Cinema can serve as an educational instrument not only to analyze the relation to the West, which is sometimes regarded as the domineering outsider, but also as a mirror for self-introspection. In other words, a large number of films have presented a critique of postcolonial African leaders in their failure to deliver on the promises of a political independent Africa. The prospect of independence had raised the hopes of the African peoples for a significant improvement from their socioeconomic conditions after colonial rule. Those hopes have been dashed for several reasons, including the consequences resulting from actions by corrupt political elites of whom filmmakers demand accountability, equal access to opportunities for personal and professional growth, and safeguards against different forms of persecution or violence. The topical treatment of corrupt political elites is present in African films such as in *Le mandat* (*The Money Order*, 1968) and *Xala* (1974) by Ousmane Sembène, and *One Step Forward: The Inside of Corruption* by Sylvestre Amoussou (2011); political violence portrayed in *Allah Tantou* (*God's Will*, 1992) by David Achkar, *Le Damier, Papa National Oyé!* (*The Draughtsmen Clash*, 1996) by Balufu Bakupa-Kanyinda, and *La nuit de la vérité* (*The Night of Truth*, 2004) by Fanta Regina Nacro; and films depicting migration as a result of government's failure to address youth unemployment such as in *Abouna* (*Our Father*, 2002) by Mahamat-Saleh Haroun and *La Pirogue* (*The Pirogue*, 2012) by Moussa Touré. As can be noticed, the nation-building paradigm has both domestic and international dimensions to its critique of practices or entities whose actions impede the socioeconomic development of African countries.

Considering the historical context of its birth and the liberation rhetoric that is often associated with the work of the first generation of filmmakers, African cinema has been categorized as part of Third Cinema by the Ethiopian film scholar Teshome Gabriel. The Third Cinema movement emerged in the 1960s and 1970s (initially in Latin America and Asia) as a form of politicized filmmaking that denounced neocolonialism and the Hollywood model as a money-making and entertainment cinema that did not bring to the fore the educational values of the medium. Under the Third Cinema movement, rejection of the systemic domination of Hollywood (aesthetics, discourse, and industry models) appears to be the common thread among African, Asian, and Latin American cinema. From a film history perspective, it can be argued that the Third Cinema fits in with a larger pattern of transnational creative movements that have revolutionized the film medium by introducing different aesthetics, as is the case with Italian Neorealism and French New Wave, with regard to on-location shooting, use of nonprofessional actors, the quotidian life, and new ways of storytelling and editing. The presence of these elements is well established in certain African films through the influence of Italian Neorealism, French New Wave, Russian Formalism, and Bollywood. But most significant is the African oral tradition that has inspired storytelling in African films and the emergence of Nollywood which provides insights into the contribution of cinemas outside the mainstream.

The presentation of the paradigms of decolonizing the gaze and nation-building, situated within the postcolonial critical framework, brings into debate the functions of film in Africa. Should African cinema be about militancy or entertainment? This is the question Congolese filmmaker Mweze Ngangura posed as he reflected in an article[1] on how to create a sustainable film industry on the continent given the scarcity of external and state funding that African cinema has long depended on for production and distribution. It is impossible to provide a straight answer to the question because of the complexities in the economics of image production and distribution globally. These issues will be addressed in detail in the following pages. Perhaps the answer to Ngangura's question is to recognize there are degrees of both militancy and entertainment in each audiovisual production and it is up to the viewer or the critic to focus on one, both, or none.

Global Positionality of African Cinemas: Ideology and Global Flows of Images

African cinema may also be read by asking where and how to situate its productions within the larger context of film as an art form. Such an interrogation aims to put cinema of the continent into conversation with the universal discourse of world cinema, highlighting differences and similarities in how it operates as an industry, produces knowledge, and engages the world. In other words, it is an approach to African cinema in relation to or in comparison with other cinematic traditions and practices around the world based on a set of parameters such as conditions of film production and distribution, structure of the film industry (vertical or horizontal organization), aesthetics, and discourse. In light of these parameters, African cinema has often been classified as belonging to broader cinema categories such as Third Cinema, cinema of the Global South, minor transnational cinema, world cinema, or what Hamid Naficy refers to as an "Accented Cinema." The common denominator among these categories resides in the fact that they all refer to productions outside popular and mainstream cinemas that are dominated by the Hollywood cinema model. The latter is a studio- and star-system industry that wields tremendous power in controlling vast networks of theatrical distribution worldwide and mobilizing funds for big-budget movies. On the contrary, African cinema is not built on the studio-system model and the star system is limited at best, with the exception of Nollywood stars. However, it should be noted that there are popular household-name actors in many countries who are generally well known to the public through their breakout roles—which often earn them the character's name throughout their professional careers. Nollywood stars have played a significant role in the industry as "icons" in the production and distribution of Nollywood films in Africa and in the diaspora (Tsika, 2015, 6), which Noah Tsika examines in his 2015 book on *Nollywood Stars: Media and Migration in West Africa and the Diaspora*. As discussed earlier, Third Cinema is a movement that encompasses productions from Latin America, Asia, and Africa featuring anti-imperialist rhetoric and offering different aesthetics from that of mainstream commercial cinema. Obviously, Third Cinema brings to mind the division of the world during the Cold War, into First World (Western Bloc and Allies), Second World (Eastern Bloc), and Third World (developing countries of Africa, Asia, and Latin America). As the Cold War came to an end in 1989 (with the symbolic fall of the Berlin Wall), anti-imperialism and the discourse of oppositionality started losing some momentum, thus the fading relevance of Third Cinema as a classificatory and analytic instrument. Like Third Cinema, cinema of the Global South also carries the idea of a distinctive separation of cinema in a tier system that is informed by the Global North's competitive edge through technological breakthroughs, funding, and better control of distribution circuits. So, the oppositionality may not be as neatly articulated as in Third Cinema, but it still looms large in the background of the interactions between the Global North and South—a political and economic dividing line between rich and poor countries. As for the term 'world cinema,' it comes across as a loosely constructed marketing categorization often used by festivals and film distributors to group productions based on their foreign origin or being outside commercial mainstream productions. Beyond the inequality dimension, the global positionality of African cinema as a form of minor cinema (production and distribution) brings to the fore the question of reading African cinema from below (Harrow, *Trash: African Cinema from*

Below, 2013) and the question of appropriation of popular entertainment film genres. How best to read African cinema based on its own creative value instead of the temptation to conflate its marginality at the global level with a possible lack of notable artistry in its works? In this context, Kenneth Harrow proposes the notion of "trash" as a critical lens through which to analyze African cinema as "a site of resistance" to hegemonic cinematic conventions (2013, 8). "Trash" is premised on the idea that there is a wealth of creativity in what may appear as low-quality productions to anyone with no knowledge of or prior exposure to African cinema. The productions have rich creative content, as evidenced by critical acclaim and festival prizes for works such as *La Noire de …* (*Black Girl*, 1966) by Ousmane Sembène, *Yeelen* (Souleymane Cissé, 1987), Idrissa Ouédraogo (*Tilaï*, 1990), *Un homme qui crie* (*A Screaming Man*, 2010) by Mahamat-Saleh Haroun, and *Félicité* (Alain Gomis, 2017).

The challenges facing African films are about better integration into the global circulation of cultural productions, visibility, and accessibility. Concerning appropriation, it "means taking a cultural form, a symbolic representation, for example, out of one context and putting it into another, whereby shifts of meaning most likely occur" (Krings, 2015, 17). The notion of appropriation could provide insights into the production and distribution of African cinema, particularly in the context of the global circulation of audiovisual images. Are the recent adaptations of popular entertainment genres such as westerns, action-thrillers, science fiction, and TV series geared toward the development of popular cinema from the art house origins of African cinema? What are the dominant thematic treatments and aesthetic constructions of these productions? Do they target local audiences or cater mostly to international audiences? In this respect, films such as *Pumzi*[2] (Wanuri Kahiu, 2009), *L'or des Younga*[3] (Boubakar Diallo, 2006), *African Cowboy* (Rodney Charles, 2013), and *Ma Famille* (*My Family*, 2002–2017) by Akissi Delta represent an illustrative corpus to study.

Gender and Feminist Readings of African Cinemas

The gender readings of African films tend to focus on women's conditions and the need to improve them by addressing forms of oppression and injustice that are undermining their socioeconomic and political situation, especially in patriarchal societies (Figure 7.1). Women's conditions are often presented against the backdrop of degrading cultural practices, the ramifications of patriarchy regarding gender roles, and the marginality of women in the screen media sector. The practices of female genital mutilation (FGM), levirate polygamy, and violations of the female body

Figure 7.1 Faat Kiné (Ousmane Sembène, 2001). Courtesy of California Newsreel.

are the subject matter of numerous films such as *Difret* (Zeresenay Mehari, 2014), *Moolaadé* (Ousmane Sembène, 2004), *Mossane* (Safi Faye, 1997), *Women With Open Eyes* (Anne-Laure Folly, 1994), *The Silences of the Palace* (Moufida Tlatli, 1994), *Monday's Girls* (Ngozi Onwurah, 1993), *Finzan* (*A Dance for the Heroes*, 1989) by Cheick Oumar Sissoko, and *Bal Poussière* (*Dancing in the Dust*, 1988) by Henri Duparc. Certain African films raise the issue of women's economic and social welfare, with girls' education[4] regarded as the remedy in *Bintou* (Fanta Régina Nacro, 2001), or laws to grant women inheritance rights after the death of their husbands as depicted in *Neria* (Godwin Mawuru, 1993). In terms of analysis, this corpus of films gives insight into the economic emancipation discourse of second-wave feminism. Alternatively, these films and all productions featuring women's conditions may be analyzed by drawing on the rich corpus of works by African female writers such as Mariama Bâ, Awa Thiam, Calixthe Beyala, Tanella Boni, and Chimamanda Ngozi Adichie. They address feminism and women's conditions from an African perspective.

In contrast to films with feminist discourse that are set in contemporary (postcolonial) times, certain films take a more deconstructive approach to the situation of African women by examining gender roles before colonialism. These films provide insightful perspective on key historical junctures and power shifts that have caused women to lose power to men. *Taafe Fanga* (*Skirt Power*, 1997) by Adama Drabo, set in precolonial Africa (the Dogon region in Mali), tells the story of women taking power in their village through the Andumbulu mask. In its social and spiritual dimensions in many West African societies, the mask serves as the intermediary between the visible world (humans) and the invisible world of gods and departed ancestors. The role of gatekeeper or intermediary confers power on whoever has the mask. The film's narrative is based on a gender reversal trope, with a comic twist at times to the unfolding events. Men assume gender roles and social norms associated with women such as cooking, caring for babies, and being submissive to the wife; while women, wearing male traditional garments, lead the village decision-making council. In other words, men are reduced to the private sphere (home) while women occupy the public sphere, in the symbolic construction and mise-en-scène of power. Having realized the potential of the mask as an instrument of power, men outmaneuver the village women to take possession of it and ensure that women will never again have access to it. This is why women and children traditionally stay indoors when those wearing masks are out performing in sacred ritual ceremonies. Drabo uses this story about the origins of the mask, predating colonialism, to point to gender construction and power dynamics in patriarchal societies.

The deconstructive approach also features prominently in African films on gender politics, particularly how women are omitted in the recording of official national histories and the collective memory of the struggle for independence in many countries. The narrative of injustice in these films showcases how women's sacrifice is not regarded as equal to men's. These films not only underline the double standard in the recognition of sacrifice along gender lines, but also appear to be aiming at rewriting history that is inclusive of all actors regardless of their gender. Productions such as Ingrid Sinclair's *Flame* (1996) and *Sambizanga* (1972) by Sarah Maldoror bring attention to stories of wartime sacrifice by African women for causes larger than themselves. *Flame* takes the viewer into the disillusionment experienced by Flame and Liberty, two women who have come to the realization that the newly independent Zimbabwe has forgotten about liberation fighters like them. They feel that they have been exploited and will have to survive by their own means. Independence has not delivered on the promises of a better future together. As for *Sambizanga*, it shows the resilience of the character Maria on a journey to find her revolutionary husband Xavier Domingos who has been jailed and is at risk of being killed like other Angolan militants fighting Portugal. The female characters of Flame, Liberty, and Maria are the unsung heroes of liberation movements that saw men and women fighting side by side on the battlefields, and yet experiencing a differentiated recognition for their service to the nation.

In addition, gender readings of African cinema have also concerned the place of women in the audiovisual industry, which is characterized by marginality in terms of the number of women directors versus men, leadership positions, and access to production resources. For her film *Tam-Tam à Paris* (1963), Thérèse Sita Bella is regarded as one of the first African female directors (Vieyra, 1968, 67) in a male-dominated medium. The situation is improving through different institutional and private initiatives, but it is still nowhere near what one would expect for a group that represents about 52 percent of the continent's population. For instance, Safi Faye, Sarah Maldoror, and Fanta Régina Nacro are among the very few female sub-Saharan African directors who have made feature-length films, with a majority of women directors making short to medium-length productions. This situation points to the larger issue of women's presence in the film industry, notably their limited access to funding and resources that would enable them to fully bring their artistic visions to the screen. The documentary *Sisters of the Screen: African Women in the Cinema* (2002) by Beti Ellerson is a good resource that introduces the viewer to African women directors and actresses in the audiovisual industry. It is important to note that obstacles have not deterred women from creative undertakings in filmmaking, which has brought about, according to Alessandro Jedlowski, a new form of economic and social mobility for many successful women in the Nigerian film industry. Successful women entrepreneurs (producers, directors, and founders of film festivals) in the Southern Nigerian video film industry such as Enem Isong, Stephanie Okereke, and Peace Anyiam-Osigwe who "were able to accomplish their achievements because of their persistence and entrepreneurial skills, rather than inherited economic and social privileges" (Jedlowski, 2015, 247). In East Africa, the director Mira Nair[5] opened a film school based in Uganda in the mid-2000s, the Maisha Film Lab, to train the next generation of filmmakers. Several emerging African female filmmakers and media artists such as Wanuri Kahiu, Fatoumata Kande Senghor, Akissi Delta, Mamounata Nikiema, Kemi Adetiba, and Hawa Essuman are redefining the field of African cinema.

Within the gender readings of African cinema, there is an emerging scholarly attention to sexual minorities, particularly the investigation of on-screen representation of homosexual characters, heteronormativity, and opposition to same-sex unions in Africa. The scholarship on sexual minorities predominantly draws on a post-1990s corpus of films that can be divided into two categories: gay films, and films on gender that have same-sex narratives as subplots such as *Karmen Geï* (Joseph Gaï Ramaka, 2001). The West African films whose subject matter is entirely focused on homosexuality include *Dakan* (*Destiny*, 1997) by Mohamed Camara,

Woubi Cheri (Laurent Bocahut and Philip Brooks, 1998), and *Law 58* (Dickson Iroegbu, 2010). In other parts of Africa, queer cinema is not present such as in films by the critically acclaimed Egyptian director Youssef Chahine that often address the topic of homosexuality, and the organization of the South African Gay and Lesbian Film Festival, Out In Africa, which was launched in 1994.

For an understanding of African film theory and criticism, and its emerging trends, alternative approaches are also equally important to be addressed, particularly collective criticism, stardom, and sub-cinema/minor international cinema.

Lindiwe Dovey's book *Curating Africa in the Age of Film Festivals* (2015) provides a fresh, new approach to African film criticism by demonstrating how film festivals, and the audience, can bring about collective criticism that emanates from conversations with the audience and critical interventions at festivals. Dovey's main argument should be understood in the context of African film criticism having mostly drawn on Western theories or relied on a single critic's/author's/scholar's conception (Figures 7.2 and 7.3).

Figure 7.2 Headquarters of the Pan-African Film and Television Festival of Ouagadougou (FESPACO). Courtesy of Boukary Sawadogo.

Figure 7.3 FESPACO mascot at the 2021 edition of the festival. Courtesy of Boukary
Sawadogo.

In the broader context of redefining film studies, works such as the
edited volume *De-Westernizing Film Studies* (edited by Saër Maty Bâ
and Will Higbee, 2012) challenge the dominant Western theoretical
frameworks.

Stardom is another emerging critical approach to African cinema, with
Noah Tsika's groundbreaking book *Nollywood Stars: Media and Migration
in West Africa and the Diaspora* (2015) on Nigerian movie stars. Not only
does Tsika provide evidence as to why stars exist, but he also addresses
the unique qualities of relevant and popular stars in Nollywood, both
individually and collectively, so as to show how significant they are both
locally and internationally. In this respect, Tsika's book certainly shares
similar aspects with Richard Dyer's star theory, which posits the star as
a construction and commodity created for financial gains. Tsika's book
provides a template for further scholarly investigations on the place and
role of stars in African film industries.

Concerning the influence of the video format and technology in
the development of industries such as Nollywood, Ghallywood, and
Bongowood, different iterations of the sub-cinema paradigm have

been used by scholars (Moradewun Adejunmobi, Alessandro Jedlowski, Carmela Garritano, Akin Adesokan, and Jonathan Haynes) to contextualize and examine the rise of these film industries. The sub-cinema paradigm, as postulated and pioneered by Roman Lobato (*Shadow Economies of Cinema: Mapping Informal Film Distribution*, 2012), is particularly applicable to how these film industries engage with the video format and technology in the production and distribution of films. The informality, cheapness, and the operation of underground pirates are all characteristic features of such a cinematic practice. Informality, accessibility, and global circulation of these video-films have been the subject of a growing corpus of writings on Ghanaian and Nigerian films: the 'televisual turn' and Nollywood as a minor transnational film industry by Moradewun Adejunmobi, and the creation of Nollywood film genres that is addressed by Jonathan Haynes.

In the conclusion to this chapter, it is imperative to also take a prospective outlook on the criticism of African cinema following the presentation of its current state (paradigms or lenses) in the scholarship. What are the emerging trends in the construction of theoretical frameworks for African cinema? The answer to this interrogation lies in the calls for new conceptual frameworks recently made by several African film scholars such as Kenneth Harrow, Manthia Diawara, and Alexie Tcheuyap. They all advocate for new critical reading lenses that move beyond the anti-colonial, nation-building, and cultural nationalism rhetoric that have been some of the most recurrent theoretical approaches to African cinema over many decades. In his latest two single-authored books, *Postcolonial African Cinema: From Political Engagement to Postmodernism* (2007) and *Trash: African Cinema from Below* (2013), Kenneth Harrow brings to the fore postmodernism and the notion of 'trash' as new critical tools. In this regard, as Harrow notes,

> It is time for a revolution in African film criticism. A revolution against the old tired formulas deployed in justification of filmmaking practices that have not substantially changed in forty years. Time for new voices, a new paradigm, a new view—a new Aristotle to invent the poetics we need for today.
>
> (Harrow, 2007, xi)

That revolution in African criticism is exemplified in Alexie Tcheuyap's book on *Postnationalist African Cinemas* (2011) where the postnationalist reading lens is offered as an upgrade to the nation-building framework. As for Manthia Diawara, in his book *African Film: New Forms of Aesthetics and*

Politics (2010), he brings a fresh perspective on African cinema by examining the continuity and discontinuity of Ousmane Sembène's influence on African cinema from the 1990s onward, thus unearthing new trends in African filmmaking. These critical endeavors are all attempting to best capture and translate the changing landscape of African cinema because of technological innovation, new forms of production and distribution, the emergence of new voices beyond auteur filmmakers, and the position of Africa within the global flows of images. The emergence of Nollywood[6] in the early 1990s is a notable change in the African cinema landscape. It is important to point out that the Nollywood model of cinema has its detractors and advocates among filmmakers and scholars. The start of Nollywood studies is credited to two books: *Cinema and Social Change in West Africa* (1995) by Onookome Okome and Jonathan Haynes, and *Nigerian Video Films* (2000) edited by Jonathan Haynes.

In addition to the previously described emerging critical lenses, I should also add that more aesthetics-centered analysis would certainly enrich the scholarship on African cinema beyond the dominant mode of textual interpretation that I referenced in the introduction to the chapter. As a relatively young field of study, there are many unexplored areas such as the intersection of art or art history with African cinema, film genre studies, and African cinema and the diaspora.

Case Study: *Atlantics* (Mati Diop, 2019): Migration in a Polygeneric Film

The Franco-Senegalese Mati Diop's feature directorial debut *Atlantique* (*Atlantics*) won the Grand Prix at Cannes Film Festival in 2019, an addition to the very short list of films by African directors which have garnered prestigious prizes at Cannes. The story in *Atlantics* is built around the coming of age of a group of young women in the Senegalese capital city of Dakar, specifically the 17-year-old protagonist Ada, who resisted a traditional marriage to the wealthy immigrant, Omar, because she is in love with a poor construction worker, Souleiman. The film offers multilayered readings and social commentary on migration, genre cinema, and the neoliberal economy, with ancillary questions of global inequalities and corruption at the local level.

The movie opens on construction workers demanding their pay of several months and then cuts to some of the construction workers, among them Souleiman, in the back of a pickup truck that is racing along the coastline. They sing to give themselves courage to keep hope, but disappointment and disillusion can be read on their facial expressions. The crooked real estate developer who failed to pay them and the general lack of upward social mobility opportunities compounded their sense of entrapment with no viable future on the horizon. To these young men, migration, however treacherous the journey might be to reach the Global North, offers some hope to build a future for themselves and their families. Dreams are broken when the young men drowned in the Atlantic Ocean en route to Spain, leaving their girlfriends devastated, as they had left without informing them or saying goodbye, which is not customary in the local culture. Emotional trauma and the burden of responsibility saddled the girls for most of the film. In some ways, *Atlantics* is also the story of those who stayed behind waiting for their loved ones who have migrated. In this respect, *Atlantics* is part of a trend, which includes the films *Les larmes de l'émigration* (Tears of Emigration, 2010) by Alassane Diago, *En attendant les hommes* (*Waiting for Men*, 2007) by Kati Lena Ndiaye from Senegal, and *Abouna* (*Our Father*, 2002) by Chadian director Mahamat-Saleh Haroun.

Atlantics may be regarded as an ode to Senegalese cinema in how it enmeshes traditions of Senegalese filmmaking, including Ousmane Sembène's sociorealist films, with a strong message against exploitation and oppression, and the oneiric world that often characterizes Djibril Diop Mambéty's films. As the plot unfolds, the polygeneric dimensions of the film become more apparent as detective fiction and zombie-like narrative take over the sociorealist vein after the moment the young men drowned in the ocean. The iconography of zombie movies in *Atlantics* features a foggy coastline, a futuristic tower, eerie music, and the night scenes when the women become their boyfriends' surrogates for justice. Boundaries are sometimes dissolved between lived reality and beyond, which is in perfect alignment with African cosmology about the visible and invisible worlds. For instance, police detective Issa had to navigate the two worlds, after initially searching for physical and rational evidence to establish the truth, in order to close the case about the fire in which Souleiman was the main suspect. The names of characters are also meaningful, as Souleiman, son of David, conveys something of master of djinns in the Qur'an while Ada means tradition in Wolof with a subtle reference to Adam.

In conclusion, here are three questions for your further consideration: How does one reconstitute history when one is disappearing or dying? Are women agents of social change from the margins in Africa? Where do you situate *Atlantics* within the larger developmental trajectory of African cinemas today?

Notes

1 "African Cinema: Militancy or Entertainment?" (1996)
2 The Swahili word for 'breath.'

3 The title may be translated in English as "The Gold of Younga Brothers."
4 Male children are often given priority in schooling decisions within traditional family structures.
5 Mira Nair is the director of the film *Queen of Katwe* (2016), set in Uganda, featuring Lupita Nyong'o and David Oyelowo.
6 Over the last few years, a number of directors have shifted from video to film for better quality and relatively big-budget productions—referred to as 'New Nollywood.'

Bibliography and Filmography

Adejunmobi, Moradewun. "Evolving Nollywood Templates for Minor Transnational Film." *Black Camera* 5, no. 2 (2014): 74–94.

Ashcroft, Bill, Gareth Griffiths, and Helen Tiffin. *The Empire Writes Back: Theory and Practice in Post-Colonial Literatures*. 2nd ed. London and New York: Routledge, 2002.

Bâ, Saër Maty, and Will Higbee. *De-Westernizing Film Studies*. New York: Routledge, 2012.

Barlet, Olivier. *African Cinemas: Decolonizing the Gaze*. London: Zed Books, 2000.

Boughedir, Ferid. "A Cinema Fighting for Its Liberation." In *Cinemas of the Black Diaspora: Diversity, Dependence, and Oppositionality*, ed. Martin T. Michael, 111–117. Detroit: Wayne State University Press, 1996.

Diawara, Manthia. *African Cinema: Politics and Culture*. Bloomington: Indiana University Press, 1992.

Diawara, Manthia. *African Film: New Forms of Aesthetics and Politics*. Munich, Germany: Prestel, 2010.

Diawara, Manthia. "The Artist as the Leader of the Revolution: The History of the Fédération Panafricaine des Cinéastes." In *Cinemas of the Black Diaspora: Diversity, Dependence, and Oppositionality*, ed. Martin T. Michael, 95–110. Detroit: Wayne State University Press, 1996.

Dovey, Lindiwe. *Curating Africa in the Age of Film Festivals*. New York: Palgrave Macmillan, 2015.

Dyer, Richard. *Heavenly Bodies: Film Stars and Society*. 2nd ed. New York: Routledge, 2003.

Flame. Dir. Ingrid Sinclair. JBA edition & Zimmedia, 1996.

Gabriel, H. Teshome. *Third Cinema in the Third World: The Aesthetics of Liberation*. Ann Arbor: UMI Research Press, 1982.

Harrow, W. Kenneth. *Trash: African Cinema from Below*. Bloomington and Indianapolis: Indiana University Press, 2013.

Haynes, Jonathan, ed. *Nigerian Video Films*. Athens: Ohio University Press, 2000.

Hoefert de Turégano, Teresa. "Featuring African Cinemas." *World Literature Today* 77, no. 3/4 (2003): 14–18.

Jedlowski, Alessandro. "The Women behind the Camera: Female Entrepreneurship in Southern Nigerian Video Film Industry." In *Cultural Entrepreneurship in Africa*, ed. Ute Röschenthaler and Dorothea Schulz, 247–263, New York: Routledge, 2015.

Krings, Matthias. *African Appropriations: Cultural Difference, Mimesis, and Media.* Bloomington and Indianapolis: Indiana University Press, 2015.

Lobato, Roman. *Shadow Economies of Cinema: Mapping Informal Film Distribution.* London and New York: Palgrave Macmillan, 2012.

Mbembe, Achille.*On the Postcolony.* Berkeley, Los Angeles, and London: University of California Press, 2001.

Ngangura, Dieudonné Mweze. "African Cinema: Militancy or Entertainment?" In *African Experiences of Cinema,* ed. Imruh Bakari and Mbaye Cham, 60–64. London: British Film Institute, 1996.

Okome, Onookome, and Jonathan Haynes. *Cinema and Social Change in West Africa.* Jos: Nigerian Film Corporation, 1995.

Ritzer, Ivo, and Peter W. Schulze, eds. *Genre Hybridisation: Global Cinematic Flows.* Marburg: Schüren, 2013.

Sambizanga. Dir. Sarah Maldoror. New Yorker, 1972.

Şaul, Mahir. "Art, Politics, and Commerce in Francophone African Cinema." In *Viewing African Cinema in the Twenty-First Century: Art Films and the Nollywood Video Revolution,* ed. Mahir Şaul, and Ralph A. Austen, 133–159. Athens: Ohio State University Press, 2010.

Solanas, Fernando, and Octavio Getino. "Toward a Third Cinema." *Cinéaste* 4, no. 3 (1970–1971): 1–10.

Taafe Fanga (Skirt Power). Dir. Adama Drabo. California Newsreel, 1997.

Tcheuyap, Alexie. *Postnationalist African Cinemas.* Manchester: Manchester University Press, 2011.

Tsika, A. Noah. *Nollywood Stars: Media Migration in West Africa and the Diaspora.* Bloomington and Indianapolis: Indiana University Press, 2015.

Young, Robert J. C. *Postcolonialism: A Very Short Introduction.* Oxford and New York: Oxford University Press, 2003.

Suggested Readings and Films

Adejunmobi, Moradewun. "African Media Studies and Marginality at the Center." *Black Camera* 7, no. 2 (Spring 2016): 125–139.

Adejunmobi, Moradewun. "Evolving Nollywood Templates for Transnational Film." *Black Camera* 5, no. 2 (2014): 74–94.

Bakari, Imruh. "African Film in the 21st Century: Some Notes to a Provocation." *Communication Cultures in Africa* 1, no. 1 (2018): 8–27.

Cinema Novo. Dir. Eryk Rocha. Icarus Films, 2017.

Donadey, Anne. "Representing Gender and Sexual Trauma: Moufida Tlatli's Silences of the Palace." *South Central Review* 28, no. 1 (Spring 2011): 36–51.

En attendant les hommes (Waiting for Men). Dir. Katy Lena Ndiaye. Néon Rouge Production, 2007.

Givanni, June, ed. *Symbolic Narratives/African Cinema: Audiences, Theory and the Moving Image,* 109–121. London: BFI Publishing, 2000.

Harrow, Kenneth W., ed. *African Cinema: Postcolonial and Feminist Readings.* Trenton and Asmara, Eritrea: Africa World Press, 1999.

Harrow, Kenneth W. *Postcolonial African Cinema: From Political Engagement to Postmodernism.* Bloomington: Indiana University Press, 2007.

Haynes, Jonathan. "What Is to Be Done?" In *Viewing African Cinema in the Twenty-First Century: Art Films and the Nollywood Video Revolution,* ed. Mahir Şaul, and Ralph A. Austen, 11–25. Athens: Ohio University Press, 2010.

Higgins, MaryEllen, Rita Keresztesi, and Dayna Oscherwitz, eds. *The Western in the Global South.* New York and London: Routledge, 2015.

Jedlowski, Alessandro. "Studying Media 'from' the South: African Media Studies and Global Perspectives." *Black Camera* 7, no. 2 (Spring 2016): 174–193.

Masilela, Notongela. "Presence Africaine and the Emergence of African Film Criticism." *Communicare: Journal for Communication Sciences in Southern Africa* 15 (1996): 1–44.

Migraine-George, Thérèse. "Beyond the 'Internalist' vs. 'Externalist' Debate: The Local-Global Identities of African Homosexuals in Two Films, *Woubi Chéri* and *Dakan.*" *Journal of African Cultural Studies* 16, no. 1 (2003): 45–56.

Naficy, Hamid. *An Accented Cinema: Exilic and Diasporic Filmmaking.* Princeton: Princeton University Press, 2001.

Palmier, Jean Joseph. *La femme noire dans le cinéma contemporain: Star ou faire-valoir?* Paris: Harmattan, 2006.

Pines, Jim, and Paul Willemen, eds. *Questions of Third Cinema.* London: British Film Institute, 1990.

Sawadogo, Boukary. *Les cinémas francophones ouest africains, 1990–2005.* Paris: Harmattan, 2013.

Sisters of the Screen: African Women in the Cinema. Dir. Beti Ellerson. Women Make Movies, 2002.

Tcheuyap, Alexie. "African Cinema and Representations of (Homo)Sexuality." In *Body, Sexuality, and Gender: Versions and Subversions in African Literatures 1,* ed. Flora Veit-Wild, and Dirk Naguschewski, 143–154. Amsterdam and New York: Rodopi, 2005.

Tcheuyap, Alexie. "Comedy of Power, Power of Comedy: Strategic Transformations in African Cinemas." *Journal of African Cultural Studies* 22, no. 1 (June 2010): 25–40.

Thiam, Awa. *Speak Out, Black Sisters: Feminism and Oppression in Black Africa.* London, Sydney, and Dover: Pluto Press, 1986.

Tsika, Noah A. *Pink 2.0 Encoding Queer Cinema on the Internet.* Bloomington: Indiana University Press, 2016.

Ukadike, Frank Nwachukwu, ed. *Critical Approaches to African Cinema Discourse.* Lanham and Plymouth: Lexington Books, 2014.

Vieyra, Paulin Soumanou. "Le film africain: d'expression française." *African Arts* 1, no. 3 (Spring 1968): 60–69.

Suggested Readings and Films

2 Weeks in Lagos. Dir. Kathryn Fasegha. 2019.
A Tale of Love and Desire. Dir. Leyla Bouzid. K Films Amerique, 2021.

Air Conditioner. Dir. Fradique. Geração 80, 2020.

An Opera of the World. Dir. Manthia Diawara. Third World Newsreel, 2018.

Borders. Dir. Apolline Traoré. DIFFA, 2018.

Harrow, Kenneth W., and Carmela Garritano. *A Companion to African Cinema*. Hoboken: Wiley Blackwell, 2018.

Nafi's Father. Dir. Mamadou Dia. JHR Films, 2019.

Night of Kings. Dir. Philippe Lacôte. Neon, 2020.

Sawadogo, Boukary. "Presence and Exhibition of African Film in Harlem." *Journal of African Cinemas* 12, no. 2–3 (2020): 163–175.

Sofia. Dir. Meryem Benm'Barek-Aloïsi. Memento Films, 2018.

Standing on Their Shoulders. Dir. Xoliswa Sithole. 2018.

The Gravedigger's Wife. Dir. Khadar Ayderus Ahmed. Orange Studio, 2021.

Tomaselli, Keyan G. "Africa, Film Theory and Globalization: Reflections on the First Ten Years of the *Journal of African Cinemas*." *Journal of African Cinemas* 13, no. 1 (2021): 3–28.

Zinder. Dir. Aicha Macky. Andana Films, 2021.

Part IV

Traditions and Practices in African Screen Media

8   Ethiopian Cinema

Steven W. Thomas

Associate Professor of English, Wagner College,
New York. USA.

Introduction—Relation to African Cinema

How Ethiopia fits into the category 'African film' is a more complicated question than it might appear at first glance. On the one hand,
Ethiopia was the host country for the Organization of African Unity,
established in 1963, that later became the African Union and that
was an early partner in the founding of the Pan-African Federation
of Filmmakers (FEPACI). Ethiopian filmmakers such as Haile Gerima,
Solomon Bekele Weya, and Abraham Haile Biru have participated in
African film festivals such as the Panafrican Film and Television Festival
of Ouagadougou (FESPACO). As one of the few countries on the continent of Africa never colonized by a European empire, Ethiopia carries a somewhat privileged position and therefore assumed a symbolic,
leadership role in the decolonization of Africa in the 1960s. But on the
other hand, precisely because it was not colonized and also because
of its proximity to the Red Sea and the Arabian Peninsula, Ethiopia
is in some ways different from the rest of the African continent. One
difference is that the Anglophone and Francophone African countries
share a common experience along with common colonial languages
and international networks that enable movies from Nigeria to be
somewhat easily enjoyed in Botswana and movies from Senegal to be
enjoyed in Chad. As the earlier chapters of this textbook point out,
they also may share an approach to cinema that aims to "decolonize
the gaze" and that reflects on the postcolonial condition. In contrast,
Ethiopian movies made in its Indigenous languages (mostly Amharic)
are somewhat linguistically isolated. Moreover, culturally, Ethiopia has
connections across the Red Sea region harkening back millennia. Its
national epic, the *Kebre Nagast* (Glory of Kings), tells of the relationship
between Ethiopia's Queen Sheba and Israel's King Solomon and how
the famous Arc of the Covenant was taken from Jerusalem to Ethiopia.

DOI: 10.4324/9781003246763-12

This biblically rooted text and the mystique of the royal family lineage have inspired a version of global pan-Africanism sometimes called 'Ethiopianism,' whose most well-known manifestation today is the Rastafarians. Ethiopia is paradoxically a representative African nation and an exception.

Hence, although one might assume that Ethiopian movies should be included in African film studies, until recently most books and scholarly journals in American and British libraries on the topic of African cinema had little to say about movies from Ethiopia. If they had anything, it was likely to be about its most famous director, Haile Gerima, who is a professor at Howard University in Washington, DC; the documentary filmmaker Salem Mekuria, who is a professor at Wellesley College in Massachusetts; and/or its most famous film theorist, Teshome Gabriel (discussed in Chapter 7), who was a professor at the University of California, Los Angeles. In contrast to the works of these three individuals based in the United States, the movies and film theory produced inside Ethiopia did not receive much international attention, not so much because of lack of interest in them but more because of lack of access to them. However, in recent years, what has changed Ethiopia's relationship to African cinema may be part of the same global phenomenon that has changed African cinema's relationship to itself—namely, the introduction of digital technologies, economic growth across the continent due to increases in foreign investments from Asia and the Middle East, and the globalization of the market for screen entertainment due to the internet and a highly networked, mobile, and cosmopolitan (or 'Afropolitan') diaspora community. Nevertheless, compared with countries such as Burkina Faso or Ghana, where individuals might somewhat casually identify themselves as "African filmmakers" in a way that transcends the particularities of their nation-state, Ethiopian filmmakers might be inclined to identify themselves as essentially Ethiopian first, and contingently African second.

Much of the scholarly work on Ethiopian cinema has begun with the question: How does its movie industry compare with that of other African countries? There are two ways to reflect on this question. One way is to think historically (or 'diachronically'), tracing the development of the movie industry and its relation to the rest of Africa. Telling the story of Ethiopian cinema in its various historical contexts is complicated because one must be mindful of how its geographic boundaries and its relationships with other African countries, Europe, and the Americas have changed over time. For instance, from 1952 to 1991, Ethiopia's territorial boundaries included Eritrea. The adjective 'Ethiopian' is somewhat fluid and could mean different things, depending on the context.

Also, like many other African countries, Ethiopia is a diverse country of many languages, cultures, and religions.

The other way is to compare and contrast ('synchronically') the diversity of new movies being produced today and the contexts for their production. One might roughly divide Ethiopian movies into three distinct categories each with a different style and relationship to other African cinema cultures. Some directors such as Haile Gerima, Salem Mekuria, Jessica Beshir, and Dagmawi Yimer live and work outside of Ethiopia. They often identify with an international black film culture and make artistically challenging, politically conscious films for a global audience (often with funding from philanthropies for the arts). A second category of Ethiopian cinema contains the big-budget multinational co-productions made in the Hollywood style by an international crew. The most successful of these is *Difret* (2014) about a heroic, feminist lawyer who defends a young girl who had shot her would-be abductor, directed by Zeresenay Berhane Mehari, whose executive producer was the American star actress Angelina Jolie. Third, inside Ethiopia, roughly 80 to 100 new feature-length dramatic movies are produced for its local theaters each year, including romantic comedies, melodramas, and historical dramas in a variety of languages, mostly Amharic, but also in Afan Oromo and Tigrinya and a mix of other languages. Most of these have been made on small budgets of roughly $15,000 to $25,000, such as the romantic comedy *YeWendoch Guday* by Henok Ayele (2007), one of the most popular movies with theater-going audiences in Ethiopia. Although frequently the low-budget local fare is criticized for being formulaic and vapid, many directors do tackle important issues with moral purpose. To name just a few, Theodros Teshome's *Kazkaza Welafen*/Cold Flame (2002) addresses the HIV-AIDS epidemic; Hermon Hailay's *Price of Love* (2015) won awards at international film festivals with its gritty and honest portrayal of the life of a prostitute and human trafficking. Kidst Yilma's *Rebuni* (2015) asserts the value of Indigenous knowledge and care for the land in the face of corporate economic development. And Sewumehon Yismawu's *Sewenetwa* (2019) is a complexly feminist film, partly funded by the International Labour Organization, that tackles the difficult subject of migration of female labor between Ethiopia and the Arab Peninsula. Significantly, many of the most impactful new local productions—e.g., *Price of Love*, *Rebuni*, and *Sewenetwa* mentioned above being just a few—are written, directed, and/or produced by women whose position in Ethiopian cinema is (one might argue) perhaps more central and less marginal than that of women in Hollywood and movie industries elsewhere in the world.[1]

Historical Contexts

At the end of the 19th century, during the infamous 'scramble for Africa,' some Europeans regarded Ethiopia—or Abyssinia as it was called then—as an exception to the rest of the continent because of its ancient Christian heritage. Following the completion of the Suez Canal in 1869, France, England, and Italy colonized the strategic coastline of the Red Sea and traded with the Abyssinian kingdoms in the highlands. The trade included European guns brought into Abyssinia and enslaved people taken out, along with commodities such as Ethiopia's famous coffee. At the end of the century, among the Abyssinian kings competing for power, Menelik II consolidated his rule and became emperor. Observing what the Europeans were doing in the region, Menelik expanded his empire into the fertile lands in the south, either through strategic alliances or violent conquest of other peoples such as the Oromo, Afar, Somali, Sidama, Wolaita, and Gurage. In 1896, his army soundly defeated an Italian invasion at the famous Battle of Adwa which inspired black people across the world. Meanwhile, around the same time as the war between Italy and Ethiopia, the Lumiere brothers in France began traveling the globe showing and making short movies. 'Cinema' had just begun. In Menelik II's palace, a French merchant showed a film in April 1897. The same year, a French company also began construction on a railway from its colony Djibouti on the coast up the mountain to Abyssinia's new capital city, Addis Ababa (New Flower). Menelik was known to have an eye toward modernizing his country, and so he encouraged foreign proprietors to establish a cinema. In response, the Orthodox Christian clergy expressed opposition and famously named the cinema *yeseytan bet*—Devil's House. One of the theaters in Ethiopia is sometimes still jokingly referred to by that nickname.

Nevertheless, despite the church's condemnation, it appeared that cinema might become popular among the urban elite. The crown prince Ras Teferi Mekonnen, who was made regent of Ethiopia in 1917 after the deposition of Lij Iasu, and then renamed Haile Selassie when he was made emperor in 1930, also had an interest in the cinema as well as in trains and motorcars. In 1923, he was the only African leader to successfully become a member of the League of Nations. Tragically, the League proved to be hypocritical and chose not to protect Ethiopia from being invaded a second time by Italy in 1935, the prelude to World War II. Italy's occupation lasted until 1941, during which time they destroyed much of what had been built, but also quickly established their own theaters. The Fascist party promoted and cultivated racist cinema about Africa in order to justify its conquest and violation of international agreements; the theaters it built in Asmara and Addis Ababa were part of its colonial project. Ethiopian resistance to the Italian occupation became legendary, and an important Ethiopian movie dramatizing this historical moment is *Ashenge* (Paolos Regassa, 2007).

As World War II came to an end, Haile Selassie returned with an eye toward modernizing the country. Theaters in Addis Ababa tended to show American movies. In 1955, he established the Haile Selassie I theater, now known as the National Theater, and two years later established the arts school at the national university. As the art historian Elizabeth Giorgis has pointed out in her book *Modernist Art in Ethiopia*, there was a tension among poets, novelists, journalists, and painters between three competing emotions: pride in Ethiopian traditions, the desire to emulate Europe, and racial solidarity with other Africans. Made in 1964, Ethiopia's first feature-length movie reflects that tension between tradition and modernity. *Hirut, abatwa mannew?/Hirut, Who Is Her Father?* is about a young woman from the country who comes to the city and is forced by socioeconomic circumstances to engage in prostitution (Figure 8.1).

It was written by Ilala Ibsa, directed by the Ethiopian-born Greek director Lambros Jokaris with a mostly European technical crew, edited in Italy, and produced by a private company in Ethiopia. That same year, the Ethiopian government also created its first television station with the assistance of the British company Thompson Television International. Four years later, Radio Ethiopia and Ethiopian Television merged into the Ethiopian Broadcasting Service, financed and tightly controlled by the government. Its weekly schedule included mostly local and international news alongside American popular movies and television shows such as *Flipper* and *Hawaii Five-O*.

Ethiopia was also sending students to universities in the United States, Europe, and the Soviet Union for education. During the final years of the emperor's reign, three students—Michel Papatakis, Getachew Desta, and Tafesse Jarra—returned from the Soviet Union with degrees in film arts and pioneered a new Ethiopian cinema. On May 17, 1974, in the Haile Selassie I theater, Michel Papatakis released what is considered the first feature-length Ethiopian movie to be produced, written, directed, and crewed primarily by Ethiopians: *Gouma*. The word *gouma* is an Indigenous concept for several ethnic groups in Ethiopia that originated from the Oromo language; the promotional poster and advertisements for the film translated the word to mean 'blood ransom,' though one could also translate it as 'reparations' or the process of reconciliation. It tells the story of a young man who mistakenly kills his best friend and therefore is required by custom to beg for money to pay reparations to

Figure 8.1 Hirut, abatwa mannew?/Hirut, Who Is Her Father? Courtesy of Steven W. Thomas.

the family of the deceased. The film was well received and highly praised in local newspapers in Addis Ababa and Asmara, and it also did well at international festivals in Tunisia and Ireland. The success of the film appeared to inspire confidence in the possibility of a local film industry, but four months after its debut screening, the emperor was deposed on September 12 by a military coup. Civil unrest over a variety of issues had reached its breaking point when news of terrible famine reached the public.

At roughly the same time that *Gouma*'s director was studying in the Soviet Union, another studied theater and film in the United States; in 1970 Haile Gerima joined a cohort of black filmmakers at the University of California, Los Angeles (UCLA), that would come to be known as the LA Rebellion (discussed in Chapter 3). Gerima arrived there at an auspicious time just one year after the famous African American philosopher

Angela Davis joined the university as a professor and just a few years before another Ethiopian intellectual, Teshome Gabriel, began his career at UCLA as one of the most important early theorists of 'Third Cinema.' All of them were part of an international movement against racism and colonialism that linked students, professors, artists, and activists from around the world. At that time, the Ethiopian Student Union of North America as well as the politically underground National Union of Ethiopian Students in Addis Ababa were inspired by Frantz Fanon and other philosophers of black liberation. Haile Gerima got permission to bring film equipment from UCLA to Ethiopia to begin filming a movie dramatizing the oppression of the peasants by the feudal landlords. Perhaps motivating his trip back to his home country was the Hollywood movie *Shaft in Africa* (released June 1973), a commercially successful movie featuring an African American private detective, much of which was shot on location in Ethiopia. Or perhaps it was something else—the documentary film *The Unknown Famine* by the British journalist Jonathan Dimbleby had shocked the world when, in October 1973, it first showed images of thousands of starving people in Ethiopia. Haile Gerima's brief sojourn home occurred at the height of political activism in Ethiopia and also just weeks after the theatrical release of *Gouma*. After shooting the film, he returned to UCLA at the end of the summer, shortly before the Emperor Haile Selassie was deposed and arrested. He completed editing his film *Mirt Sost Shi Amet/Harvest: 3000 Years* the following year at the same time that he was working on another film, *Bush Mama*, that dramatizes the radicalization of an African American woman in Los Angeles after her husband returns from the Vietnam War, experiences racism in America, and is wrongly imprisoned.

The deposition of Haile Selassie in 1974 created a power vacuum. The Ethiopian student movement that had led the revolution divided into factions over disputes over issues of socialist doctrine, including the issue of the right to self-determination by the various nations, nationalities, and peoples within Ethiopia. Into that power vacuum, the military 'Derg' regime stepped in with a nominally communist mandate. By 1977, Ethiopia had shifted its military alliance from the United States to the Soviet Union. The period under the Derg was simultaneously productive and repressive. It was productive in the way it extended university education and other opportunities to women and instituted the Ethiopian Film Center in 1978, which eventually became the Ethiopian Film Corporation in 1986. Young film students had opportunities to train and participate in film festivals in the USSR and Nigeria with other students from Latin America, Asia, Europe, and Africa. The government saw film as a tool of the revolutionary movement and therefore initially emphasized creative documentaries that were made in multiple languages in order to reach different ethnic groups and that celebrated socialist struggle; these included *3002: Wondimu's Memories* (Teferi Bizuayehu, 1976) and *Tiggil Dil, Dil Tiggil/Struggle Victory, Victory Struggle* (Michel Papatakis, 1978). However, the Derg was also harshly repressive of dissent and enforced an ideological discipline that discouraged creative and commercial efforts.

Conflict between political factions led to the infamous 'Red Terror' when in 1976–1977 the Derg government killed an estimated 60,000 people and tortured many more. Ethiopia is still recovering from the psychological and economic trauma of the Red Terror and the civil war that eventually led to the overthrow of the Derg in 1991. Thereafter, many filmmakers have attempted to come to terms with it, including in the movies *The Father* (Ermias Woldeamlak, 2000), *Qey Sihtet/ The Red Mistake* (Theodros Teshome, 2006), *Siryet* (Yidnekachew Shumete 2007), *Lomi Shita/*Scent of Lemon (Abraham Gezahegn, 2008), and *Taza/*Threshold (Kidist Yilma, 2016). The most famous of these is Haile Gerima's internationally acclaimed *Teza/*Morning Dew (2008), which will be described in more detail later in this chapter. These movies evoke the message now etched in stone outside the Red Terror Museum in Ethiopia's capital city: "never ever again." The Ethiopian-Israeli filmmaker Aäläm-Wärqe Davidian focuses on how Ethiopian Jews (known as 'Beta Israel' in Ethiopia) experienced the conflict in her movie *Fig Tree* (2018). Two documentary films about this time period are *Ye Wonz Maibel (Deluge)* (1997) directed by Salem Mekuria and *Finding Sally* (2020) directed by Tamara Mariam Dawit. As Bitania Tadesse has argued, such films ideologically encode both public memory of the past and national feelings about the future of the country.[2]

In addition, one of the outcomes of the civil war and change in government in 1991 is that Eritrea elected to separate from Ethiopia in 1993. Eritrea was an Italian colony from 1889 until the defeat of the fascists in World War II, and before that, from the 17th through the 19th centuries, much of its coastline was controlled by the Ottoman Turkish Empire. From 1950, it was federated with Ethiopia, and indeed its capital city Asmara, with its many movie theaters, paralleled Addis Ababa as a cultural center.[3] Movies made at this time reflected this geography. For instance, the 1964 movie *Hirut* ends with its protagonist moving from Addis Ababa to Asmara. Consequently, today, when one speaks of "Ethiopian cinema," one is usually referring to cinema produced within the boundaries of the Ethiopian state constitutionally determined in 1993, but it is important to keep in mind that cinema production and consumption before that year included audiences and artists from Eritrea as well.

During the final years of the Derg regime, two fictional dramas were produced by the Ethiopian Film Corporation: *Behiwot Zuria* (Berhanu Shiberu, 1989) and *Aster* (Solomon Bekele Weya, 1991). Both films aim at raising consciousness of economic class disparities and show a cross section of different aspects of Ethiopian society. *Aster* is about the daughter of a factory worker who marries a doctor who falls in love with her while she is a patient in his hospital. Tragically, she experiences class prejudice and social discrimination, leading to a startling and unresolved conclusion. In many ways, Ethiopia's cinema history and its political history are connected in ways similar to those of other African countries during the Cold War. Between the United States and Western Europe on one side and the Soviet Union on the other, African filmmakers felt caught between the opportunities and the limitations of both. Ethiopia was no different in that respect. Then, after the Cold War ended and global financial institutions and lenders such as the IMF began a period of "structural adjustment" and "austerity" measures that reduced public spending on the arts, the movie and television industry floundered for much of the 1990s. Ethiopia's government had to figure out a new economic model and was perhaps somewhat unique for charting a middle way forward where the "activist developmental state" synthesized socialist nation building with capitalist, entrepreneurial development.[4]

What was also new for Ethiopia in the 1990s was a government interested in fostering a multicultural, pluralistic state that—at least in constitutional principle if not always in practice—respected the right of self-determination for its diverse nations, nationalities, and peoples. The principle of self-determination that was so important for the decolonization of Africa in the 1960s and 1970s had also led to various liberation movements in Ethiopia (e.g., Eritrean People's Liberation Front, Oromo Liberation Front, Tigray People's Liberation Front), which aimed to revolutionize the Ethiopian constitution in 1992. What this meant for the film and television industries was that now there were television programs in other languages than Amharic, such as Afan Oromo, Somali, and Tigrinya. However, for much of the 1990s, television dramas failed to impress audiences, government censorship persisted, and the limited number of theaters showed mostly Hollywood and Bollywood movies.

But this changed in 2002, when theaters for the first time exhibited three movies shot on VHS, rather than on the traditional and more expensive celluloid: *Kazkaza Welafen*/Cold Flame (Theodros Teshome), *Gudifecha*/Adoption (Tatek Tadesse), and *Yeberedow Zemen*/Ice Age (Helen Tadessa). Following the surprising success of these movies, local theaters realized they could actually make a lot of money from cheaply produced, local movies that represented the lives of their audiences. Very soon after, cinema across the world made the switch from celluloid to digital, and at the same time, the economy of Ethiopia began to grow rapidly, spurred by foreign investment in new forms of industry that encouraged migration to cities. Local movie production in Ethiopia exploded. Because creative young people were excited to make movies, short technical courses began to be offered at videography schools such as the Tom Photography and Videography Training Center, Master Films and Communications, and the Blue Nile Film and Television Academy.

The task among scholars and students of African film studies has been how to understand this new kind of cinema experience. Initially, both journalists and scholars compared Ethiopia's new video-film industry to Nigeria's "Nollywood." However, while there are some similarities, there are also some differences. The primary difference is that Nollywood movies in the late 1990s and early 2000s were straight-to-video, where VHS, DVD, and VCDs were quickly copied, marketed, and distributed to be watched primarily at home or in small video parlors. Much of the early video market in Nigeria was what economists call "informal" (or black market and off the books), where piracy was the norm. In contrast, in Ethiopia distribution was primarily to movie theaters, many of which were still government owned, and all movies had to be licensed by the government. Whereas the Nigerian model reflected the context of neoliberal capitalism partly dominated by European corporations, the Ethiopian model reflected the context of state socialism where the government protected locally owned industries and where many of the film and media professionals were on government salaries. Hence, the Ethiopian model was a hybrid of entrepreneurial ingenuity to raise enough money to make a movie and government control of the market. The rapid growth in the movie industry led to the creation of the Ethiopian International Film Festival in 2005, the Gumma film awards in 2014, and a master's degree program in film at Addis Ababa University in 2015. Historically, Ethiopia's movie industry has undergone many changes, and one might anticipate yet another change since the increase in internet and cell phone use has diverted attention toward other screen media such as Facebook and YouTube.

Case Studies: Haile Gerima's *Teza* (2008) and *La Borena* (Belay Getaneh, 2013)

Choosing a single movie to represent the variety and diversity of films in Ethiopia for this textbook is somewhat difficult. Ethiopia's most famous director is Haile Gerima, who is known for making artistically innovative and politically provocative films. He is also known for maintaining total control over the production and distribution of his work in order to achieve the utmost artistic integrity. However, within Ethiopia since 2005, a popular commercial cinema has emerged that connects with local audiences. Although many are somewhat formulaic rom-coms and soap-opera-like melodramas, some raise profound questions about the human psyche, such as *Meba* (Kidist Yilma, 2015) and *Emnet* (Arsema Worku, 2016), while others imaginatively probe the possibility of Ethiopia's political future, such as *Etege II* (Abiy Fanta, 2010), *Utopia* (Behailu Wassie, 2015), and *Sost Maezen 2* (Theodros Teshome, 2016). Moreover, some draw from works of modern Ethiopian literature, such as the award-winning *Lomi Shita* (Abraham Gezahign, 2011), adapted from a novel by Adam Reta, that has a complex nonlinear narrative structure to present a multifaceted view of Ethiopian identity and history. A third category of Ethiopian cinema includes multinational co-productions aimed at mainstream global audiences; these films include *Lamb* (Yared Zeleke, 2015) and *Sweetness in the Belly* (Zeresenay Berhane Mehari, 2020, starring American and British movie stars Dakota Fanning, Wunmi Mosaku, and Yahya Abdul Mateen II).

For the sake of addressing some of the central themes of African Film Studies, I have chosen two that raise some of the questions discussed elsewhere in this book: *Teza* and *La Borena*. Haile Gerima's *Teza*/Morning Dew (2008) is an obvious choice because it is the most internationally acclaimed Ethiopian film, winning best picture at FESPACO and at the Carthage International Film Festival. With funding from multiple sources such as the European Union Commission, its budget was roughly €400,000. In contrast, *La Borena* (Belay Getaneh, 2013) is more typical of the hundreds of romantic comedies and melodramas that have been made in Ethiopia with small budgets around $20,000. But as typical as *La Borena* is in some ways, it is also unusual in that the road-trip story takes the characters out of the capital city to the pastoral region in the far south. The self-consciously cross-cultural plot opens the audience to Ethiopia's ethnic diversity, and at the same time, the character of a white anthropologist reframes some of the questions asked in other chapters of this book about the relationship between the European anthropologist and the colonialist gaze upon the ethnic 'other.'

Haile Gerima's films are part of an international black filmmaking tradition. He was a member of what has been labeled the 'LA Rebellion,' a group of filmmakers at UCLA, including African American directors Julie Dash and Charles Burnett, and he has been teaching at the historically black Howard University in Washington, DC. Many of his films are about the African American experience in the United States. As Chapter 3 of this textbook discusses in detail, African American and African filmmakers shared common ground in forging and theorizing an anti-racist approach to filmmaking, and they often inspired each other's work. Haile Gerima has frequently acknowledged his debt to Ousmane Sembène, once remarking, "I am a Sembene soldier. I believe in Sembene and his work showed me the way."[5] For many African Americans with an interest in politically engaged cinema about racial issues, Haile Gerima's most famous movie is *Sankofa*, regarded as one of the best movies dramatizing slavery and the transatlantic slave trade. Many of his other movies, such as *Bush Mama* (1976) and *Ashes and Embers* (1982), engage with the political issues important for African Americans, such as the Vietnam War, the American criminal justice system, and, of course, racism. He also has made two documentaries about Ethiopia history: *Imperfect Journey* (1994) and *Adwa: An African Victory* (1999).

Teza is a complex movie that weaves together the history of political conflict in Ethiopia with the African experiences of global racism. The movie's arrangement is nonlinear as it moves back and forth between different moments in time to evoke the fragmented, disjointed memory of the psychologically and physically traumatized protagonist Anberber. Anberber's story begins when he is studying microbiology in Germany and also participating in the Ethiopian student movement advocating for the democratization of Ethiopia and economic justice for the peasant and working classes. His friend Tesfaye marries a white woman, Gaby, despite prophetic warnings from Anberber's bi-racial girlfriend Cassandra that their child will suffer in a racist Germany. After Haile Selassie is overthrown, Anberber and Tesfaye return to Ethiopia hoping to contribute to a new society. However, when conflicts between factions ensue and the chaos of the Red Terror grows worse, Tesfaye is killed and Anberber becomes a target. Partly for his safety, the government relocates him back to Germany to continue his scientific work there. Before Anberber can inform Gaby and her son of Tesfaye's death, he is attacked by racist German thugs and left severely crippled. He then returns to Ethiopia feeling psychologically and physically lost to discover that both the Derg regime and EPRDF rebels are forcefully recruiting boys from his family's village to fight. This story is narrated in flashbacks, as if the movie is putting together pieces of traumatic memory. Meanwhile, the past in Germany and the past during the Red Terror are both repeatedly juxtaposed with Anberber's present, as he tries to figure out who he will become back home while the civil war continues around them and as his new lover is ostracized from the village. Village politics in some ways mirror national politics. The movie concludes hopefully with Anberber finding a calling and his lover giving birth.

It is a challenging film for many reasons. One reason is the richness of its allusions to Ethiopia's history and culture, including religious symbols, art, folk songs, and literature. Moreover, the film also resonates with a broader African history, including the struggle to build a decolonized nation and the cultural displacement of the revolutionary intellectuals, alienated from the people whom they aim to serve. A second reason consists of the many narrative threads woven together as the film reassembles the pieces of Anberber's memory. One might be tempted to focus on just one of these threads, such as his experience of racism, the implosion of the Derg's nation-building program into a violently repressive state, his alienation from his homeland and its traditions, or the cultural life of his home during the civil war. However, Haile Gerima's use of nonlinear plotting, crosscutting between historical moments, and montage technique to juxtapose and weave all of these threads together invites the audience into an open-ended exploration of how the events in one time and in one place relate to those in another time and place. Attending to the many provocative juxtapositions, one might ask what does the weight of all this history mean for the individual, and how can one resurrect one's sense of moral and political purpose?

One might also compare the fictional and experimentally nonlinear movie *Teza* to the documentary films *Sidet: Forced Exile* (1991) and *Ye Wonz Maibel (Deluge)* (1997) by Salem Mekuria. Like Gerima, Mekuria came to the United States as a student in the late 1960s; she remained in the United States to eventually become a college professor, and, in addition to making movies about Ethiopia, she also makes movies about the African American experience, such as *Our Place in the Sun* (1988) and *As I Remember It: Portrait of Dorothy West* (1991).[6] Mekuria's film *Sidet* is about refugees who fled the Derg regime and the civil war in Ethiopia to Sudan. Focusing on the lives of several women, her film moves far beyond the media stereotype of the refugee to reveal the diversity of experiences of those who labor to maintain themselves and their children in difficult circumstances in Sudan. Her film highlights the precarious situations of women who, at the time she made the film, were often overlooked in male-centered narratives about African refugees. How these working women and caregivers experience 'forced exile' is clearly different from the form of exile that Anberber experiences as a scientist in *Teza*. Her next movie, *Deluge*, takes a more personal approach to the subject of the political conflicts that led to the Red Terror as Mekuria makes her own life story and role as a filmmaker a part of the film. *Deluge* begins with a dedication to her brother Solomon, her close childhood friend Negist, and the "tens of thousands who lost their lives for their ideals." In many ways, the film is an attempt to come to terms with how her brother and best friend came to be on opposing sides and how they died. Solomon was committed to the Ethiopian People's Revolutionary Party (EPRP) that was opposed to the military Derg leadership, while Negist was in the All Ethiopia Socialist Movement (MEISON) that chose to make a tactical alliance with the Derg. Between 1976 and 1978, at the height of conflict between these two socialist parties, thousands were assassinated and tortured. Families and friends were suddenly deeply divided. Like Gerima's *Teza*, Mekuria's *Deluge* reframes the international media's coverage of this conflict from the perspective of an Ethiopian in exile. But unlike in *Teza*, in which the main character is a scientist who tried unsuccessfully to avoid factional politics and was antagonized by those whose motivations in the film are unsympathetic and unclear, about *Deluge* Mekuria explicitly says that she wants to find a way to understand what may have motivated her brother and her friend to take their opposing positions while acknowledging her own geographic distance from their situation.

In stark contrast to *Teza* and *Deluge*, the movie *La Borena* (Belay Getaneh, 2013) is an entirely different sort of movie in terms of its conception, story, style, and production. It is a romantic comedy about a tour driver named Tewedros (Tedy) who is hired by a young anthropologist from France named Zoe Salvage to take her to the Borana region. Eventually they fall in love. Although her professional purpose is to study the Borana for her PhD dissertation, her personal motivation is that her father spent years in the Borana region and died there at the same time she was born. In many ways, the movie is typical of the romantic comedy genre and begins like many other Ethiopian movies when a young aspiring working-class Ethiopian loses a girlfriend or boyfriend to a wealthier foreigner with promises of a better life in America. Other romantic comedies similarly stage the problem of love confronting a disparity in wealth and reflect on the position of Ethiopia in the global economy. One example is the influential *YeWendoch Guday* (Henok Ayele, 2007), a movie that self-consciously alludes to the popular American rom-com *Wedding Crashers* (David Dobkin, 2005). Such movies comment critically on the shallow materialism that motivates desire for America. A common plot in Ethiopian movies features characters from different socioeconomic backgrounds finding a truer love, sometimes by rediscovering core values or their Ethiopian-ness. Related to this theme is the country-city dynamic, exhibited in sweetly sentimental movies such as *Laundry Boy* (Leul Solomon and Tsegaye Yohannes, 2010), in which urban Ethiopians rediscover their true selves by returning to their roots in the country. Considering the rapid growth of Addis Ababa and other

cities in recent years due to migration from the country to the city, perhaps these movies speak to nostalgic feelings their audiences may have
for a more authentic Ethiopia that they feel they are losing as the city
globalizes. In addition, such films participate in the postcolonial political project of African cinema to "decolonize the mind" by critiquing
the fetishization of American-style consumer capitalism. What makes *La
Borena* somewhat unique in Ethiopian cinema is how this return to the
country happens at the southern border of Ethiopia, as the movie dramatizes an encounter with the exotic 'other' within Ethiopia's boundaries,
the Borana Oromo who famously still practice an Indigenous form of
democratic culture hundreds of years old—the Gadaa system.[7]

The film is complex in its mixing of themes. This is especially evident in terms of how the filmmakers from Addis Ababa appropriate the
European anthropological gaze (the character of Zoe) as a vehicle for
their own gaze on a minority ethnic group at the border, where the
Borana continue to govern themselves with their own form of law. The
border zone is cinematically transfigured into a place where true love and
human values can be discovered and reclaimed. On the one hand, what is
refreshing about *La Borena* is its positive representation and pride regarding Ethiopia's ethnic diversity. This includes allusions ranging from the
Amhara Emperor Tewedros's resistance to European colonialism to the
Oromo Gadaa system of democracy. On the other hand, the idealization
and exotification of the Borana Oromo as geographically distant and
culturally outside Ethiopia's mainstream political system somewhat elides
the more politically difficult presence of Oromo closer to and within the
nation's urban centers such as Addis Ababa, Jimma, Ambo, Dire Dawa,
and Adama.

The movie is in some ways similar to, and in other ways different
from, how the films of other countries have wrestled with the European
anthropological gaze on Africa as an exotic 'other.' As discussed in early
chapters of *African Film Studies*, African filmmakers from Safi Faye to
Souleymane Cissé have pioneered an African cinema that (in the words
of film studies theorists such as Manthia Diawara and Olivier Barlet)
"decolonizes the gaze," by presenting an alternative African subjectivity.
Their 'decolonizing' alternative reflects on tradition as dynamic rather
than static; it presents multiple and complex points of view rather than
cartoonishly flat and singular caricatures; and it looks forward to a better
sense of self, while being conscious of how colonialism has shaped and
transformed those traditions and subjectivities. Decolonizing the gaze
means resisting and deconstructing the discourses of European colonialism (e.g., the discipline of ethnography and anthropology) that essential-
ized and racialized African cultures as premodern and in need of Europe's

civilizing mission. Ethiopian cinema clearly shares that sense of Africa cinema's frustration with its position in the global economic order and its exotification by Western media. In one scene in *La Borena*, Tedy gets angry with Zoe for her assumptions about Ethiopian poverty, and he points out the moments in history when Ethiopia gave aid to Germany and Japan. Ethiopia differs from other African countries in that it was not colonized by Europe, so one might also point out that the dominant nations and nationalities of Ethiopia (namely the Amhara and Tigray ethnic groups) in some ways occupy the historical position of the colonizer of the other nations, nationalities, and peoples of Ethiopia such as the Borana Oromo.

There are several questions that *La Borena* opens up for discussion. One is how the movie may or may not position the urban audience of Addis Ababa watching the film as a confidant of the European anthropologist, watching the other cultures of their country through her eyes. She literally has the "last word" in the movie when her voice-over narrative concludes, "Ethiopia is in God's hands, that's my last word." In what way is the movie's celebration of diversity and difference a form of inclusion and in what way might it also be a subtle form of exclusion? A second question is whether her statements about Ethiopia are meant to confirm how the Ethiopian audience feels about themselves or whether such statements ironically mimic the ways a white European might (incorrectly) think about Ethiopia. Arguably, what makes it an interesting and successful film is that it leaves these questions open.

A third question is how the movie's representation of the Borana Oromo compares to movies made by Oromos about themselves. Oromo filmmakers have also attempted to "decolonize the gaze," which for them partly means gaining the recognition from the world that they exist. Facing the erasure of some of their culture, Oromo filmmakers have made films and written novels that recuperate traditions such as the Gadaa system and Indigenous forms of women's empowerment. How well does *La Borena* contribute to this cultural project? Although one might criticize its representation of the Borana for being somewhat exotified and idealized, some of the Oromo movies such as the short films *Qanafaa* (Tura and Dibisa, 2015) and *Gumaa* (Kumsa Tamana, 2016) also paint idealized pictures of Oromo traditions. Other Oromo films and television such as the popular TV drama *Dheebu* (Kelbessa Mergessa, 2015–2017) and the first Oromo feature drama *Eelaa* (Abraham Jalata, 2005) instead aim to adapt these traditions to modern life, focusing on relations between the country and the city and between the rich and the poor, in ways quite similar to the mainstream Ethiopian movies in the Amharic language.

Figure 8.2 Faya Dayi (2021) by Jessica Beshir. With permission of Jessica Beshir.

A strikingly original and unique new film is Jessica Beshir's documentary *Faya Dayi* (2021) that has won many awards for its complex portrait of Oromo farmers and laborers of the Hararghe region involved in the khat trade. It is the first film in the Oromo language to be so internationally exhibited and acclaimed. It is an observational documentary of startling intimacy set in and around the ancient Islamic city of Harar, but it is also a visual poem that weaves together stories of different young men and women, reflections on the Oromo Protest Movement, and the Islamic Sufi rituals and mythologies around the narcotic khat plant. In its weaving together these stories, it evokes a spiritual, dream-like transcendence as it probes the dreams of young men and women for a better life (Figure 8.2).

Of course, not all filmmakers and films signal their ethnic identity or foreground traditional cultures. In fact, many theater managers in the big cities believe the formula for a commercially successful movie is one that reflects the globally hybrid culture of urban life and that might appeal to as broad an audience as possible no matter what their background— e.g., slapstick comedy and love triangles. Point being, ultimately there are many different kinds of Ethiopian cinema to be enjoyed for different reasons. The ongoing questions that continue to interest scholars who situate Ethiopia's movie industry within African film studies are many, from the changing modes of production and the relationship to the state to how certain film genres encode various ideologies, cultures, and social issues.

Notes

1 Eyerusaleam Kassahun, "Women's Participation in Ethiopian Cinema," in *Cine-Ethiopia: The History and Politics in the Horn of Africa*, ed. Michael W. Thomas, Alessandro Jedlowski, and Aboneh Asahgrie (East Lansing: Michigan State

University Press, 2018), 119–140; Steven W. Thomas, "The Women Blowing Up Ethiopia's Film Industry," *Zócalo Public Square* (September 11, 2020), https://www.zocalopublicsquare.org/2020/09/11/women-ethiopian-film-industry-rukiya-ahmed-helen-tadesse-arsema-workukidist-yilma/ideas/essay/.
2 Bitania Tadesse, "Revolutionary Ethiopia through the Lens of the Contemporary Film Industry," *Northeast African Studies* 16, no. 1 (2016): 167–196.
3 Jane Plastow, "Teatra Asmara," *Journal of African Cultural Studies* 29, no. 3 (2017): 311–330.
4 Steven W. Thomas, "Theorizing Globalization in Ethiopia's Movie Industry," *Black Camera* 11, no. 2 (2020): 60–84.
5 Tekletsadik Belachew, "The Dead Speaking to the Living: Religo-Cultural Symbolisms in the Amharic Films of Haile Gerima," in *Cine-Ethiopia: The History and Politics in the Horn of Africa*, ed. Michael W. Thomas, Alessandro Jedlowski, and Aboneh Asahgrie (East Lansing: Michigan State University Press, 2018), 68.
6 Nwachukwu Frank Ukadike, Interview with Salem Mekura, in *Questioning African Cinema: Conversations with Filmmakers* (Minneapolis: University of Minnesota Press, 2002), 239–251.
7 Perhaps the most famous anthropological study of the Borana is by the Eritrean anthropologist Asmerom Legesse, *Gada: Three Approaches to the Study of African Society* (New York: Free Press, 1973).

Further Reading

Jedlowski, Alessandro. "Screening Ethiopia: A Preliminary Study of the Contemporary Developments of Film Production in Ethiopia." *Journal of African Cinemas* 7, no. 2 (2015): 169–185.
Kassahun, Eyeruseleam, and Steven W. Thomas. "Early Ethiopian Cinema, 1964–1994." *African Studies Review* 65, no. 2 (2022): 308–330.
Plastow, Jane. "Teatro Asmara." *Journal of African Cultural Studies* 29, no. 3 (2017): 311–330.
Tadesse, Bitania. "Revolutionary Ethiopia through the Lens of the Contemporary Film Industry." *Northeast African Studies* 16, no. 1 (2016): 157–197.
Thomas, Greg, ed. "Close-up: Teza." *Black Camera* 4, no. 2 (2013): 38–162.
Thomas, Michael W. *Popular Ethiopian Cinema: Love and Other Genres.* London: Bloombury Academic, 2022.
———. "The Local Film Sensation in Ethiopia: Aesthetic Comparison with African Cinema and Alternative Experiences." *Black Camera* 7, no. 1 (2015): 17–41.
Thomas, Michael W., Alessandro Jedlowski, and Aboneh Ashagrie, eds. *Cine-Ethiopia: The History and Politics of Film in the Horn of Africa.* East Lansing: Michigan State University Press, 2018.
Thomas, Steven W. "Theorizing Globalization in Ethiopia's Movie Industry." *Black Camera* 11, no. 2 (2020): 60–84.

9 Nollywood

A Popular and Commercial Cinema

Nigerian Cinema before Nollywood

Looking at Nigerian cinema before Nollywood provides a more complex picture beyond the Nollywood film industry, which has often today become synonymous or interchangeable with the many other traditions and practices within the larger umbrella of Nigerian cinema. Under colonial rule, short educational and propaganda films were made by the Nigerian Film Unit (created in 1949) as part of the larger framework of the Colonial Film Unit (1939–1955) established by the British government. In addition to the Nigerian Film Unit, the church as an institution also played a role in film exhibition, as was the case in several other African countries under colonial rule. All these instances, again much like in other parts of the continent at the time, should be regarded as African experiences of cinema, since colonized Africans lacked the agency to be in front of and behind the camera, because they were hampered by colonial decrees (Laval Decree of 1934, for instance) meant to prohibit access to and use of film medium by Indigenous people given its transformative power. It should be noted that well before the introduction of cinema, popular forms of entertainment with traveling theatrical companies existed, which had some influence on storytelling and the aesthetics of the celluloid films of the 1960s–1990s, the videofilms of early Nollywood in the 1990s, and then the New Nollywood's productions of the mid-2000s–2010s.

Fincho (1957) by Sam Zebba is considered the first Nigerian film shot in color. The Nigerian cinema landscape would significantly change in the 1970s and 1980s, driven by the oil boom and the Indigenisation Decree in 1972 under president Yakubu Gowon. The first generation of postcolonial Nigerian filmmakers includes Ola Balogun, Hubert Ogunde, and Eddie Ugboma. Balogun's filmography features productions such as *Amadi* (1975), *Ajani Ogun* (1976), *A Deusa Negra* (Black Goddess) in 1978,

DOI: 10.4324/9781003246763-13

Cry Freedom (1981), *Orun Mooru* (Heaven Is Hot) in 1982, and *Magic of Nigeria* (1993). Eddie Ugboma's films include *Rise and Fall of Oyenusi* (1977), *The Mask* (1979), *Oil Doom* (1981), *The Boy Is Good* (1982), *Death of a Black President* (1983), and *America or Die* (1996). Other notable directors of the first two decades of post-independence Nigeria include Adamu Halilu (*Shaihu Umar*, 1976), Jimi Odumosu (horror film *Evil Encounter*, 1980), and Ngozi Onwurah (*Coffee Coloured Children*, 1988, and *The Body Beautiful*, 1990). Generally, financial resources from the oil boom have contributed to increased production of film and television content and the public having disposable income to go to the movies. As for nationalization of film theatrical distribution, similar patterns were observed in other countries such as Burkina Faso, Benin, and Senegal as part of what is commonly referred to as the cultural nationalism of newly independent African countries to develop policies and initiatives to take ownership of infrastructures (movie theaters) and narratives.

Accessibility of copies of these films remains, however, a problematic issue to contend with. Copies of old films have been lost or destroyed due to poor storage and archiving practices. Restored copies from the 35 mm or 16 mm original negatives are not always available either. In some cases, copies are held by private and public organizations in the Global North which own distribution rights over these films through funding mechanisms. The restitution of copies of old African films is the new frontier in debates on the restitution by the West of African cultural productions, after the recent restitution of African artifacts by Western museums to countries such as Senegal and Benin.

Nigeria has also contributed to nascent African film criticism, specifically through J. Koyinde Vaughan's early publications, such as his article "Africa South of the Sahara and the Cinéma" (1957) and his book chapter "Africa and the Cinema" (1960). Early African voices on African cinema in the 1950s and 1960s include Senegalese Paulin Soumanou Vieyra and various contributions on African film–related news published in the South African *Drum Magazine*.

What Is the Nollywood Model and What Was the Beginning of Nollywood Like?

Nollywood, today's mainstream Nigeria film industry, was launched in the early 1990s with the film *Living in Bondage* (Chris Obi Rapu, 1992) which is widely regarded as its foundational production. Nollywood can be defined as a film industry, primarily based in southern Nigeria, that used video technologies to revolutionize production, distribution, and reception of audiovisual stories—known in Africa and in the diaspora by different names such as home videos, home movies, or videofilms. These productions are mostly in Yoruba and/or English languages, as opposed to Kanywood, which is the Hausa-language productions from northern Nigeria. The commercial and popular success of these video-based productions is evident in other countries such as Bongowood in Tanzania, Ghallywood in Ghana, and Riverwood in Kenya. However, it is important to note the significant evolution in Nollywood developmental history from poorly scripted and shot films mostly distributed through pirated DVD copies in Africa and the diaspora to aesthetically and thematically well-articulated stories screened in modern movie theaters, distributed through online platforms and on cable television (Multichoice, Canal+Afrique, StarTimes, and Disney+). In addition, Nollywood has, since the late 2010s, entered into many co-production and distribution agreements with American tech giants Netflix and Amazon. In efforts to capture and explain all the shifting landscape of Nollywood film industry, scholars and film industry professionals have sometimes used terms such as New Nollywood and neo-Nollywood. Nollywood, already more than 30 years old, is bound to undergo further changes as it continues to develop.

As a mostly commercial and popular cinema model, Nollywood releases about 2,500 films every year, according to the 2021 UNESCO report, *The African Film Industry: Trends, Challenges and Opportunities for Growth*. This is a big film industry that has evidently shown that money can be made for those working in the sector, and also evidence to African policymakers and investors who have traditionally remained reluctant or skeptical about investing in creative cultural productions on the continent, hence the perennial question of funding (model) in African cinema. Nollywood was birthed at the confluence of the need to tell local stories and the business acumen of the storytellers. Though the self-taught makers of video or home movies did not have good command of cinema grammar, they responded in a timely way to Nigerians wanting to see their stories on screen from their own perspectives. And the popular and commercial success reached beyond Nigeria. From the home video mass-producing director Chico Ejiro in the early days of Nollywood to popular actress Genevieve Nnaji's performances to today's big budget and refined productions, Nollywood films have evolved and always found their audiences. From videotapes, VCD, DVD, theatrical distribution to streaming, Nollywood movies are circulating far and wide. Productions such as *The Figurine* (2009) by Kunle Afolayan, The *Wedding Party* (2016) by Kemi Adetiba, *Lionheart* (2018) by Genevieve Nnaji, and *The Delivery Boy* (2019) by Adekunle Adejuyigbe showcase the diversity in Nollywood film genres (Figure 9.1).

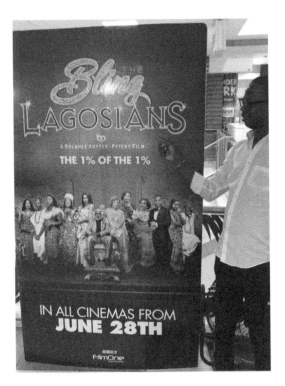

Figure 9.1 Poster of *The Bling Lagosians* at a shopping mall movie theater in Lagos, June 2019. Courtesy of Boukary Sawadogo.

Nollywood exemplifies a creative economy built from the ground up by the movie industry stakeholders themselves without government intervention. As such, it shows the feasibility, resilience, and success of a model that is different from the one that is driven and mostly funded by the government. In itself, the government-driven and funded model beyond its regulatory role is not inherently an inoperative one because it has produced results elsewhere. Besides, how much and often is governmental intervention needed or required for local, sustainable film industries in Africa to emerge, specifically in socioeconomic contexts where everything is branded as a priority by political leadership, which has kept the sector of culture severely unfunded? Very few African countries have allocated a minimum of 2 percent of their budgets to culture. In addition to the Nollywood model, there exist other models in different parts of the continent, underlining diversity in cinematic traditions and practices.

What Is the Future of Nollywood?

Nollywood continues to develop, as evidenced by further iterations of transnationalization, including, on the one hand, co-production and distribution deals with Netflix, Amazon, and Disney+, and on the other hand, the growing reach of Nollywood in the African diaspora to immigrant communities in the Global North and black audiences in the Caribbean and South American countries.[1] Transnational televisual distribution of Nollywood movies continues as many private TV stations on the continent usually have a Nollywood channel that broadcasts Nigerian films dubbed in European languages such as in French-speaking West African countries. Online platforms such as irokotv | NOLLYWOOD YouTube channel, and yes, illegal postings on digital platforms continue to contribute to the circulation of Nollywood movies. In addition, the cultural vibrancy of Nigeria on the global stage could further benefit Nollywood, ranging from literature (Chimamanda Ngozi Adichie, Nnedi Okorafor), urban naja music (Wizkid, Davido, Burna Boy) to Hollywood actors of Nigerian descent (David Oyelewo, Cynthia Erivo, Chiwetel Ejiofor).

Figure 9.2 The Lekki-Ikoyi Link Bridge features in several Nigerian movies. Photo taken in June 2019. Courtesy of Boukary Sawadogo.

As for film studies, Nollywood studies continues to grow within the larger field of African film and media studies, with growing scholarly publications and conferences. Critical interventions on Nollywood enrich conversations and reflections on African cinema.

It is important to note that Nollywood has its detractors, denouncing poorly constructed stories, limited command of film language by some directors, and enormous yearly output of films. These criticisms mask the issue of limited royalties paid to directors who are tricked into signing long-term distribution contracts with transnational media companies[2] (Figure 9.2).

Is the Nollywood Model Replicable?

Popular and commercial success has raised questions about whether Nollywood can be replicated elsewhere in Africa. Here are some responses to this interrogation.

First, Nollywood has inspired other African countries to develop local film industries, creating local stories for local audiences by taking advantage of accessible video and digital technologies for production and distribution. For instance, Ghallywood in Ghana, Riverwood in Kenya, and Bongowood in Tanzania. In terms of content, there is a remarkable development in several African countries of genre cinema—comedies, thrillers, westerns—and television serials and shows since the 2000s, bearing some influence from Nollywood.

Second, there is the view that Nollywood (success) is inherent to the socioeconomic situation of Nigeria, so it is difficult to successfully use the template in other countries. The country represents a sizable market as the most populous African country with 215 million people as of 2022, and millions more Nigerians living outside the country. Also, the existence of local structures of consumption from the long tradition of Yoruba theater means that Nollywood has something to draw on. The star system has contributed to the transnationalization of Nollywood, with a growing popularity driven by the familiar faces of such movie stars as Genevieve Nnaji, Osita Iheme, Chinedu Ikedieze, Sam Lovo Efe, Sola Sobowale, and Richard Mofe-Damijo.

Third, there are other models in Africa besides Nollywood. There is the North African model built around national cinema centers, which serve as regulatory and funding bodies, including the Centre Cinématographique Marocain of Morocco and Centre National du Cinéma et de l'Image of Tunisia. Similarly, from the mid-2000s onward, there have been film funds created by several West African countries to foster the emergence of local, sustainable film industries such as in Senegal (FOPICA), Burkina Faso (FDTC), Côte d'Ivoire (FONSIC), Ghana's National Film Authority and the Film Fund created in 2016, and the Code of Film and Animated Image passed by the parliament of Togo in September 2021. The Moroccan model, selected here as an example in North Africa, features state funding mechanisms through the Centre Cinématographique Marocain and the well-established distribution and training infrastructure of film schools and movie theaters. Three or four feature films were released annually in the early 2000s, and Morocco has now tripled or even quadrupled its annual output. Also, Morocco is one of the very few African countries that actively contribute to the emergence of the still underdeveloped practice of studio filmmaking on the continent. The Atlas Film Studios in Ouarzazate is the site of big budget foreign movies that have filmed on location, including *Lawrence of Arabia, Star Wars, Prince of Persia, The Mummy, Gladiator,* and *Game of Thrones.*

The other models concern South Africa with its historic close connections to Hollywood, with movies such as *Black Panther* (Ryan Coogler, 2018) and *The Woman King* (Gina Prince-Bythewood, 2022) featuring black and African experiences that are shot on location in South Africa. As for Egypt, it is the oldest film industry in Africa and is mostly oriented toward Arab and Middle Eastern countries in terms of content and distribution networks. But that has not always been the case historically, because Egyptian films were distributed in sub-Saharan Africa from the 1960s to the 1980s under its revolutionary and pan-African regimes. Since the first edition of the Luxor African Film Festival in February 2012 and the Alexandria Short Film Festival becoming Alexandria International Short Film at its eighth edition in February 2022, sub-Saharan African films are getting presence and attention in Egypt.

Case Study: *The Wedding Party* (Kemi Adetiba, 2017): Owambe Movies and New Approaches to Studies of Film Reception in the Era of Online Platforms

The Wedding Party's storyline is about Dunni Coker, an art gallery owner in her twenties, marrying her entrepreneur lover Dozie. Conflicts arise as the two affluent families from different backgrounds compete for who gets to make key decisions about the wedding. Secrets are revealed, promises turned out to be hard to keep, family bonds are tested, and surprises and humorous moments serve as comic release in the film narrative. *The Wedding Party* is part of Owambe movies.

The Yoruba word 'Owambe' means big parties involving food, music, and dancing to celebrate a milestone in life. Nollywood Owambe movies refer to productions featuring big parties with the drama and twists accompanying preparations and unfolding of the event itself. *The Wedding Party* (2016) by Kemi Adetiba and its sequel *The Wedding Party 2: Destination Dubai* (2017) can be regarded as Owambe movies, just like other Nollywood wedding films such as *It's Her Day* (2016) by Aniedi Awah Noba and *Two Brides and a Baby* (2011) by Teco Benson. The tradition of wedding films is not uniquely Nigerian nor a recent trend, as evidenced by Bollywood movie scenes of lavish wedding ceremonies or American comedies around weddings. The originality of *The Wedding Party* franchise, if it can be referred to as such with its sequel *The Wedding Party 2: Destination Dubai*, on the one hand resides in its contribution to the comedy genre through a star-studded cast as a form of popular and commercial cinema, and on the other hand showcases the cultural wealth and depth of Nigeria through costumes, music, food, and rituals.

The popular and commercial success of Nollywood movies such as *The Wedding Party* and many others calls for new approaches to studies of film reception in the era of online and social media platforms. Traditionally, a measure of film reception in the industry includes revenues from ticket sales at the box office, which in the case of *The Wedding Party* (2016) has reportedly made at least ₦600 million ($1.5 million) at the box office from its ₦60 budget ($150,000). TV ratings, interviews, festival awards, reviews published by scholars and critics are the other instruments to gauge and study film reception by the audience. However, there are new forms of popular engagement with digital content distribution and consumption, including likes, comments, tags, shares, reshares, clips shared via WhatsApp, illegal postings—all of which call for expanded reading tools for film reception beyond the old, tried formulas. In certain cases, for instance, Netflix algorithms and YouTube studio analytics for creators could provide equally significant insightful data to consider.

Notes

1 Sophie Collins, "Explained: Inside Nollywood, the Fastest Growing Film Industry in the World," https://movieweb.com/nollywood-film-industry/.
2 Olivier Barlet, *Contemporary African Cinema* (East Lansing: Michigan State University Press, 2016), 344.

Bibliography and Filmography

Barlet, Olivier. *Contemporary African Cinema*. East Lansing: Michigan State University Press, 2016.

Black Goddess, or A Deusa Negra. Dir. Ola Balogun. Embrafilme and Afrocult Foundation, 1978.

Coffee Coloured Children. Dir. Ngozi Onwurah. Women Make Movies, 1988.

Collins, Sophie. "Explained: Inside Nollywood, the Fastest Growing Film Industry in the World." https://movieweb.com/nollywood-film-industry/. Accessed 3/18/2022.

Evil Encounter. Dir. Jimi Odumosu. 1980.

Halilu, Adamu, dir. *Shaihu Umar.* ArtMattan Productions, 2019.

The Body Beautiful. Dir. Ngozi Omwurah. Women Make Movies, 1990.

UNESCO. *The African Film Industry: Trends, Challenges and Opportunities for Growth.* Paris: UNESCO, 2021.

Vaughan, J. Koyinde. "Africa and the Cinema." In *An African Treasury: Articles, Essays, Stories, Poems by Black Africans,* ed. Langston Hughes, 89–120. New York: Crown, 1960.

Vaughan, J. Koyinde. "Africa South of the Sahara and the Cinéma." *Présence Africaine,* no. 14/15 (1957): 210–221.

Suggested Readings and Films

2 Weeks in Lagos. Dir. Kathryn Fasegha. 2019.

Afolabi, Taiwo, and Tunde Onikoyi, eds. *The Cinema of Tunde Kelani: Aesthetics, Theatricalities and Visual Performance.* Newcastle upon Tyne: Cambridge Scholars, 2021.

Bakari, Imruh. "African Film in the 21st Century: Some Notes to a Provocation." *Communication Cultures in Africa* 1, no. 1 (2018): 8–27.

Brown, H. Matthew. *Indirect Subjects: Nollywood's Local Address.* Durham: Duke University Press, 2021.

The Bling Lagosians. Dir. Bolanle Austen-Peters. Netflix, 2019.

Tsika, Noah. *Cinematic Independence: Constructing the Big Screen in Nigeria.* Oakland: University of California Press, 2022.

10 The Rise of Local African TV Serials

The Cases of Burkina Faso and South Africa

The fastest growing sectors in the African screen media landscape today include TV serials, animated films and series, and gaming. They have yet to garner sustained scholarly attention through publications or to be the subject matter of undergraduate courses in which African popular art forms and their patterns of consumption and delivery platforms are discussed as a way to better grasp different facets of contemporary Africa. This short chapter on African TV seriality is meant to serve as a quick introduction to locally produced African TV series, shows, sitcoms, and soap operas. First, the chapter addresses the historical context of the emergence of the early locally produced serials by citing examples from Burkina Faso and South Africa, and then examines today's intervention of cable television and US tech and entertainment media giants in Africa, and finally offers a course syllabus proposal for instructors.

Until the mid-1990s, foreign television series or telenovelas dominated African national television's prime-time programming. A shift occurred in the 1990s as a result of the revolution of video and digital technologies, demands for increased local content in TV broadcasting, and the emergence of independent television rivaling the once monopolistic national TV broadcasting corporations. In terms of technological development, digital terrestrial television has expanded television coverage to the remotest areas in many African countries, with more affordable options for viewers. Digital terrestrial television has also facilitated transnational circulation of films and TV programming beyond the national scope and borders to which several African national radio and TV broadcasting corporations, created in the immediate aftermath of political independence from the late 1950s to the 1970s, had long been confined. The growth of pay television in Africa with cable and satellite television should also be noted; South African Multichoice (20.1 million subscribers), Chinese StarTimes (7.8 million subscribers), and French Canal+ (six million subscribers) are leading this market segment on the continent.[1]

DOI: 10.4324/9781003246763-14

In Burkina Faso, the first locally produced comedy TV series *À Nous la vie* (1998) and *Kadi Jolie* (1999) were made by the award-winning film-makers Dani Kouyaté and Idrissa Ouédraogo, in contrast to nowadays, when young and self-taught creatives are the ones driving productions. Following the golden decades of Burkinabe cinema from the 1980s to the 1990s, film funding became scarce and televisual productions were an option to consider for filmmakers. The state radio and television broadcasting corporation Radiodiffusion Télévision du Burkina and French CFI Television co-produced and broadcast the series. This was a time when independent television stations were not much of the landscape in Burkina Faso. Similarly, in South Africa, the first local television series were made in the 1990s when the South African television industry saw the launch of Digital Satellite Television (DStv) in 1995 and eTV in 1998 in a media landscape that the state broadcasting corporation, South African Broadcasting Corporation (SABC), had long dominated. These changes were happening in the larger historical context of the end of apartheid and the election of Nelson Mandela as president in 1994. The first locally made and broadcast South African TV series included *Generations* (1993) by Mfundi Vundla, *Isidingo* (1998) by Raymond Sargeant, and *Yizo Yizo* (1999) by Angus Gibson and Teboho Mahlatsi.

The shift to digital terrestrial television from analog television broadcasting and the corporate intervention of streaming giants in Africa have significantly changed the landscape of distribution and exhibition of films and TV serials on the continent since the 2010s. The changes bring into focus questions of copyright, ownership, and the viable economic models for screen media production and distribution in Africa. From their initial roles as distributors, several of the transnational media companies have also increasingly become producers and funders of content, strengthening their grip on different parts of the production and distribution chain of African audiovisual content. That is the case of Netflix, Disney+, Amazon, Canal+, and TV5Monde. The French Canal+, through its Abidjan-based subsidiary A+, which was created in 2014, is co-producer, funder, and distributor of a large segment of French-speaking African serials, which are made in such a formatted content that they often lack diversity and nuances beyond national or local settings. In addition, TV5Monde, the French-language cable television that broadcasts on several continents, is also a major funder and distributor of African serials.

Netflix's first African original series *Queen Sono* (2020) and *Blood and Water* (2020) both set in eastern and southern African countries, followed by *Young, Famous & African* (2022) set in Johannesburg, exemplify the shift from distributor to producer. Other Netflix African original series projects in other countries will be released by the time you are reading this book, cementing a practice. Locally produced serials for primarily local audiences such as *The Wife* (2021), a Showmax original telenovela released in 2022, are particularly appealing to viewers for relatability with the on-screen stories told in African languages other than English. The booming of serials on the continent is evidenced by the launch in 2018 of the "Série Series" pan-African festival, by Issaka Sawadogo, Oumar Dagnon, and Bénédicte Lesage, alternating between Burkina Faso and a different African country every two years.

In the context of scarcity of funding, serials offer creatives a means of sustainability for production of relatively low-budget content and for themselves a source of income. In certain cases, revenues from serials are invested toward cinematic projects. It must be acknowledged, however, that criticisms are often leveled at serials producers for being mostly driven by financial gains, which can be observed in poorly scripted stories. In other words, TV serials are often just another means to make money. In other cases, criticism takes the form of generational conflict between established filmmakers and young creatives who are harnessing new possibilities afforded by technological innovations in the creation and distribution of audiovisual content. The African screen media landscape will continue to undergo changes with the development of multiplatform entertainment and the emergence of new voices and faces of creators.

Funding and Distribution of TV Serials in Africa

Here is a list of some organizations that fund and distribute TV serials or shows in or about Africa. Many of these funding and distribution organizations are increasingly overlapping today whereby they are funders, producers, and distributors of content.

Funding Organizations of TV Serials or Shows in Africa

Netflix
Amazon
Disney+
Fonds de Promotion de l'Industrie Cinématographique et Audiovisuelle (FOPICA), Senegal
Fonds de Soutien à l'Industrie Cinématographique (FONSIC), Côte d'Ivoire
Fonds National de Développement Culturel, Togo
Fonds de Développement Culturel et Touristique (FDCT), Burkina Faso

Centre Cinématographique Marocain (Moroccan Center for Cinema),
 Morocco
Centre National du Cinéma et de l'Image (National Center of Cinema
 and Image), Tunisia
Tunisian Ministry of Cultural Affairs
National Television Broadcasting Corporations
A+, French Canal+'s African subsidiary (Côte d'Ivoire)
Showmax
Africa Magic Channel
Fonds Image de la Francophonie, International Organization of
 Francophonie
TV5Monde
European Union–Africa Caribbean Pacific (ACP)
Fonds Cinéma du Monde
Independent production companies
Doha Film Institute (Qatar)
Red Sea Fund (Saudi Arabia)

Distribution Channels of African TV Serials or Shows

Netflix
Disney+
National Television Broadcasting Corporations
South African Broadcasting Corporation
TV5Monde
Showmax
Africa Magic Channel
Independent television channels
A+, French Canal+'s African subsidiary (Côte d'Ivoire)
YouTube
Vimeo
Amazon

Course Syllabus Proposal

African Televisual Seriality: Cultural Proximity and Transnationalization

Course Description

Until the mid-1990s, Western television serials dominated African
national television's prime-time programming. A shift occurred in the
late 1990s toward locally produced TV serials, as part of the revolution

of video and digital technologies and the demand of audiences for local content. Satellite television channels, online streaming platforms, and informal distribution channels have allowed locally produced serials to reach local audiences and the African diasporic communities.

Course Objectives

- Rethink the media theory of uses and gratifications in the context of the rise of televisual seriality in Africa;
- Examine and understand the changing landscape of screen media in Africa as a prolongation and reflection of global shifts;
- Analyze the production, distribution, and reception of local television serials.

Note

1 UNESCO, *The African Film Industry: Trends, Challenges and Opportunities for Growth* (Paris: UNESCO, 2021), 7.

List of series and texts from which to select course materials

Adejunmobi, Moradewun. "African Film's Televisual Turn." *Cinema Journal* 54, no. 2 (2015): 120–125.

An African City. Dir. Nicole Amarteifio. YouTube, 2014.

Barlet, Olivier. *Contemporary African Cinema.* East Lansing: Michigan State University Press, 2016.

Ebrahim, Haseenah. "Cinematic Sidestreams: A Political Economy of Small Cinemas in South Africa." *Communicatio* 46, no. 3 (2020): 20–42.

Haynes, Jonathan. *Nollywood: The Creation of Nigerian Film Genres.* Chicago: University of Chicago Press, 2016.

Jaji, Tsitsi, and Lily Saint. "Introduction: Genre in Africa." *Journal of Postcolonial Literary Inquiry* 4, no. 2 (2017): 151–158.

Jedlowski, Alessandro. "Studying Media 'from' the South: African Media Studies and Global Perspectives." *Black Camera* 7, no. 2 (2016): 174–193.

La Pastina, C. Antonio, and Joseph D. Straubhaar. "Multiple Proximities between Television Genres and Audiences: The Schism between Telenovelas' Global Distribution and Local Consumption." *Gazette: The International Journal for Communication Studies* 67, no. 3 (2005): 271–288.

Ma famille (My Family). Dir. Akissi Delta. LAD Production, 2002–2007.

Maîtresse d'un homme marié (Mistress of a Married Man). Dir. Kalista Sy Diop. 2019 and 2020.

Moyer-Duncan, Cara. *Projecting Nation: South African Cinemas After 1994.* East Lansing: Michigan State University Press, 2020.

Queen Sono. Netflix. 2020.

Savage Beauty. Netflix, 2022.

Sawadogo, Boukary. "Are Sitcoms the Future of Francophone West African Cinemas?" *CineAction* 94 (Summer 2014): 40–44.

———. *West African Screen: Comedy, TV Series, and Transnationalization*. East Lansing: Michigan State University Press, 2019.

Straubhaar, D. Joseph. "Beyond Media Imperialism: Assymetrical Interdependence and Cultural Proximity." *Critical Studies in Mass Communication* 8 (1991): 39–59.

Tampy Police Station [Commissariat de Tampy]. Dir. Missa Hebié. 2006–2008.

The Wife. Showmax. 2021.

UNESCO. *The African Film Industry: Trends, Challenges and Opportunities for Growth*. Paris: UNESCO, 2021.

Uzalo. Dir. Gugulethu Zuma-Ncube and Dua Ndlovu. 2015.

Young, Famous & African. Netflix. 2022.

Part V

Notes on Streaming

11 The Streaming Rush for Africa

If the Western rush for extraction of African minerals and natural resources is well established in the public discourse, the streaming rush for Africa has only started to gain momentum recently.

Global Shifts in Film and Media Landscape

Larger shifts in film and media distribution globally are fast changing, from delivery platforms to consumption patterns. For instance, the once industry norm of a 90-day exclusive theatrical window in the United States has shortened by half, whereas in certain cases movies are simultaneously released in theaters and on streaming platforms, if not exclusively on streaming platforms such as Netflix productions or Warner Bros. Discovery's streaming service with HBO Max. Over-the-top (OTT) media service, delivering content directly to consumers via the internet, is expanding. These sweeping changes are driven by video and digital technological innovations and the transnational reach of US tech and media entertainment giants. For the continent of Africa, in its diverse film and media traditions and practices, these changes not only call for a rethinking of the economics of the image and media—what is the best economic model?—but also addressing opportunities and challenges for African creatives. The streaming market in Africa features several transnational media companies, including Showmax, Netflix, Apple, Amazon Prime Video, Disney+,[1] and MUBI.

The shift to digital terrestrial television from analog television broadcasting and the corporate intervention of streaming giants in Africa have significantly changed the landscape of distribution and exhibition of films and TV serials on the continent since the mid-2000s. According to the UNESCO report, released in October 2021 and titled *The African Film Industry: Trends, Challenges and Opportunities for Growth,*[2] South African Multichoice with 20.1 million subscribers,

DOI: 10.4324/9781003246763-16

Chinese StarTimes with 7.8 million subscribers, and French Canal+ with six million subscribers are leading this market segment on the continent. The COVID-19 pandemic has accelerated the pace of sweeping changes, with the ripple effects of pandemic lockdown-induced binge watching, which has further affected modes and formats of film and media consumption even in countries with fewer official reported COVID cases such as in Africa. The South Africa-based video on demand service Showmax and the American companies of Netflix, Disney+, and Amazon Prime Video are not only providing streaming services but have also contributed to ushering in a new era for African cinema in terms of economics. The intervention of Netflix, Amazon Prime Video, Disney+, and Apple Studios has so far taken the form of exclusive licensing deals of movies that already had cinema runs, multiproject development, and production of African originals in collaboration with African directors and studios. Film and television projects range from historical drama to action series to animated series. Serialization of content is one of the characteristic traits of these streaming giants for their subscription-based economic model, which is certain to have an impact on aesthetics, form, and format across productions.

Growth Potential and Challenges in Africa

The growth potential of the African media market is immense, prompting ever-increasing significant creative productions and business investments by local stakeholders and foreign companies. Africa is a market of 1.4 billion consumers as of 2022, with two-thirds the continent's population under 30 years of age. Netflix keeps expanding its footprint on the continent through content production in addition to distribution, which the streaming giant has long been associated with. Showmax is available in 45 out of 54 countries in Africa, offering films and serials in several African languages. Besides streaming, theatrical distribution also continues to be active amid the often contradictory pulses of movie theater renovations and closures in Africa. For instance, Ciné Burkina and Ciné Neerwaya in Ouagadougou, Burkina Faso, are full to capacity whenever locally made films are shown. A visitor to Lagos Island in Nigeria is pleasantly surprised at the number of fully equipped multiplexes in operation. The chain of Canal Olympia movie theaters in francophone African capitals has been part of the landscape since the 2010s. Parallel distribution networks developed by business-savvy young people are also diversifying and complexifying the practice of film exhibition. These young entrepreneur-directors organize showings of their films in villages and midsize cities in Burkina Faso, bypassing theatrical and streaming distribution outlets. Similar patterns exist in other African countries.

The intervention of streaming companies in African film and media landscape presents both opportunities and challenges for African creatives. Netflix could bring global exposure and funding opportunities through licensing deals, direct commitment to supporting the emergence of local sustainable film industries, and production of originals such as *Queen Sono* (2020) and *Blood and Water* (2020), or Netflix's Nigerian original series *King of Boys* (2021) and *Blood Sisters* (2022). Similarly, Showmax brings local stories and realities to the screen for African audiences, including its reality show *The Real Housewives of Lagos* (2022). However, streaming services in Africa still face challenges regarding consumer experience and the question of what would be the best economic model. Among those challenges are the lack of transnational payment infrastructure, getting more users into the habit of paying for online content, reliable electrical grid, and slow and expensive internet. Another obstacle is that most of Netflix Africa's originals (films and series) are not always readily available to subscribers on the continent, echoing and accentuating an old pattern of Global North-oriented distribution of African cinema, which further alienates Africans from content on or about Africa and home-grown content. Also, African film and television stakeholders now face the responsibility of successfully leveraging the intervention of these global media industry giants in Africa for the emergence of sustainable local industries through investment in infrastructure, human capital development, and a thriving economic model. If not, this streaming rush will be just another example of extraction of resources and creativity from the continent for capitalist gains. Are African countries content-producing or content-consuming countries, or both in equal measures? Certain streaming companies have recently started programs designed to train creative talents on the continent, including the launch, in early 2022, of the Netflix Creative Equity Scholarship Fund with an investment of $1 million to train film and television students in sub-Saharan Africa, starting with the Southern African Development Community (SADC) region. Are such initiatives designed to be a creative pipeline for content by Africans or just another self-serving corporate marketing strategy, or is it a mutually beneficial commitment to education for the performing arts? It is relatively early to critically assess the long-term commitment of these training initiatives or the structural impact of such programs in building local, sustainable African film and television ecosystems.

Beyond Streaming

Alternative Financial Technologies

African cinema is constantly shifting, as evidenced by streaming and televisual and theatrical distribution channels with underlying questions of funding and economic model. In this respect, African cinema should experiment with new funding and distribution models, specifically with alternative financial technologies such as nonfungible tokens or NFTs, which have so far gained more interest in the art and music worlds than in cinema.

Restitution

Ancillary to the question of distribution is the issue of circulation and accessibility to African film heritage by creatives, scholars, and cinematheques and educational institutions on the continent. Thousands of copies of old African films are held, copyrighted, and/or owned by Western production companies and public institutions through funding mechanisms. Some Western universities have acquired African cineastes' archives or collections of papers, which further raises the issue of accessibility for continental interested parties. The debate on restitution is finding its way to African cinema after the arts.

Notes

1 https://african.business/2022/03/apo-newsfeed/disney-sets-18-may-2022-as-launch-date-for-south-africa/.
2 UNESCO, *The African Film Industry: Trends, Challenges and Opportunities for Growth* (2021), 7.

Conclusion
Film and New Media Education

With the digital technological innovations and explosion of new media productions, film is no longer the only primary mode of audiovisual storytelling. A filmmaker is traditionally defined as someone who makes feature films both fiction and/or nonfiction. Today, anybody who is capable of producing moving images with sound could be regarded as a filmmaker, considering that the history of early cinema features short productions in length similar to what we currently see across multiplatform production and consumption. Early cinema productions are not the refined works that we have come to associate with today's films. The question is whether those capable of producing moving images with sound want to make it a profession or remain as amateurs. It is, however, true that cinema has its own language and that is the reason why we can understand cinema in any language. The extent to which the cinematic language is mastered is the key factor in addressing the fast-dissolving boundaries between film and new media productions.

The larger question for film educators is what skills to teach students today that they will continually use over the next decades during their filmmaking careers. The question is particularly relevant in the current context of the ubiquitous presence of images in our daily lives, in the production and distribution of audiovisual content on over-the-top (OTT) platforms, YouTube, Instagram, Meta (Facebook), Vimeo, or TikTok. Film training programs should, if not already undertaken, expand to cater to demands in video games, coding, and animation. As writing courses have long been considered foundational in academic success across fields, possessing skills in movies or video in the future will have a similar impact on success in academe (across fields and tracks) and the professional worlds. This is a mode of communication that an entire generation has already grown up using, so film educators have to keep in mind the shift and its percussions on pedagogy.

Index

Note: Page numbers in italics indicate figures.

166   *Index*

For Product Safety Concerns and Information please contact our EU
representative GPSR@taylorandfrancis.com Taylor & Francis Verlag GmbH,
Kaufingerstraße 24, 80331 München, Germany

Printed and bound by CPI Group (UK) Ltd, Croydon, CR0 4YY
08/06/2025
01897000-0009